PRAISE FOR *LIVE BY YOUR DREAMS*

Dreams are important as guidance for our lives. That is the message that author Arthur Strock teaches us in this sensitive and meaningful book. I was touched both by the meaning Arthur found in such a wide variety of dream experiences as well as his innate kindness and wisdom as a storyteller. Certainly his background as a psychologist gives him the understanding of how to work with people, but it is his natural curiosity and knowledge in dream interpretation that makes this book so special. You will enjoy reading it cover-to-cover or just picking it up to enjoy a story or two.

—Meredith Young-Sowers, D.Div.
Stillpoint School of Integrative Life Healing
Author of *Agartha* and *The Angelic Messenger Cards*

Dream sharing has been widely practiced by indigenous people over the millennia, but is a rare occurrence in modern societies. Arthur Strock's delightful book *Live By Your Dreams* hopes to reverse this trend. He compares dream sharing to story telling, but these stories contain messages that vary from dreamer to dreamer. The conversational style of this book makes it reader-friendly, even when synchronicity, premonitions, and posttraumatic stress disorder nightmares are the topic of the conversation. Many books about dreams have been published in recent years, but *Live By Your Dreams* is in a category of its own.

—Stanley Krippner, Ph.D., Saybrook University
Coauthor of *Extraordinary Dreams and How to Work With Them*

Arthur Strock is a gifted storyteller. He conveys people's dreams so eloquently that readers will be excited to turn the page and see how each event plays out. Strock's intuition and wisdom are embedded in each narrative; he has an ability to get to the heart of each person's life and how it plays out in their dreams. Strock's chapter devoted to children's dreams is invaluable, as young people's voices go relatively unheard in most dream literature. Here he captures children's waking and dream worlds—their wonderings and fears—and shows how the two realms interrelate in a clear and captivating way.

In so doing he also reminds us of how easy it is to miss the beauty of children's dream lives. This is a compelling, beautifully crafted and insightful book that will be read from cover to cover and revisited many times.

—Kate Adams, Ph.D.
Bishop Grosseteste University, Lincoln, UK
Author of *Unseen Worlds: Looking Through the Lens of Childhood*

Prior to reading Arthur's book there were three books that had influenced the course of my life and my thoughts of self and family. These books include Teillard de Chardin's *The Phenomenon of Man*, Kahlil Gibran's *The Prophet*, and Jean-Dominique Bauby's *The Diving Bell and the Butterfly*. I add this book to my list and now there are four influential books that I will read again and again! Arthur's dream insights speak to the mindfulness that is critical to a successful career and meaningful life experiences. Knowing Arthur and now reading his book have made a positive and significant influence on who I am as a person and as a professional. This book offers the reader an avenue to explore the sense of one's inner peace. Thank you Arthur for writing this book and making a positive impact on my life!

—Jane Jameson, M.S.
Superintendent, Mount Arlington Public Schools, New Jersey

Thank you Arthur for offering your unique approach to educating us about the ways we can come to understand and appreciate the value of dreams in our lives.

—Robert Gongloff, Ph.D.
Past President, International Association for the Study of Dreams
Author of *Dream Exploration: A New Approach*

LIVE BY YOUR DREAMS

*Heartwarming Stories About Dreams
and What They Tell Us*

First Printing December 2015
ISBN: 978-0-9965458-0-8
Printed in the United States of America

www.livebyyourdreams.com

LIVE BY YOUR DREAMS

*Heartwarming Stories About Dreams
and What They Tell Us*

*Roberta,
wishing you the best dreams
have to offer. With gratitude
and love.
Arthur*

11-30-16

Arthur Strock, Ph.D.

Illustrations by Giora Carmi

Prospect Park Press
West Chesterfield   New Hampshire

DEDICATION

This book is dedicated to my life partner Susan Dingsor.

Even before we met, we bumped shoulders in a dream from which I awoke experiencing the amazing and incomparable feeling of unconditional love. Years later, I continue to thank God for the depth and beauty of her love, a love that is life sustaining.

ACKNOWLEDGEMENTS

A huge, well-deserved, and heartfelt thank you to all of the dreamers who took me into their confidence and shared their dreams and stories with me. Special thanks to Andre, Juan, and Jordan for giving me the first dream story to be written for this book. I know how much you wanted your real names to appear in this book. You got your wish.

Many thanks to my daughter Shannon whose love, admiration, and continued dream sharing I value beyond measure.

A big thank you to Jo Ann Kuruc, who somehow knew the day we met that I needed to study dreams and told me to do so, while providing me with a simple prescription for dream recall. Father Al Gorayreb deserves a great deal of credit for teaching me, and many others, the basics of dreamwork. Henry Reed is greatly appreciated for sending me an invitation to become a founding member of the International Association for the Study of Dreams, an invitation I gratefully accepted. Thanks to Mark Thurston for his life-changing course at Atlantic University on how to teach dreams. Thanks to Joan Heleine for her support. Thanks to Leslie Ellis for sharing the results of her research on the treatment of repetitive nightmares.

Thanks to Mike Reed and colleagues at Prospect Communications for removing roadblocks to publication. In less than an hour of our first meeting, they had uncovered my lost website that had been hacked and destroyed. Mike also had wonderful suggestions regarding the title of the book and the format. Subsequent contacts showed Mike's patience in dealing with my most elementary questions.

Thanks to Barbara Wright for her years of ongoing support, compliments on my early writing, and the assurance that I had something to say.

Thank you Roberta Ossana for graciously writing such an insightful foreword for this book. Thank you Giora Carmi for your visually appealing and emotionally engaging illustrations that add greater depth of insight to the stories. Although I no longer laugh and cry as I did looking at them for the first time, I continue to enjoy them with a sense of wonderment. Thank you Cindy Seelig for your input regarding titles and book appeal. Thank you Kate Adams, John Ermanis, Robert Gongloff, Jane Jameson, Stanley Krippner, Frank Pascoe, Henry Reed, Kevin Todeschi, Robert Waggoner, and Meredith Young-Sowers for taking time out of your busy schedules to review and endorse the book prior to publication.

It is with ongoing gratitude that I thank Meredith Young-Sowers for her years of supporting my personal growth through her Stillpoint Institute programs and her tireless hours upon hours of editing this book. Her knowledge of dreams, creative suggestions, and devotion to the project have resulted in a book of far greater value than I could have written without her help. A portion of the proceeds of this book will go to support her Stillpoint Foundation.

Thank you Susan for helping when I asked and for allowing me space when I needed it. Thank you so much for being you in spite of dealing with job stress that is clearly world class. Most of all, I thank you for helping provide the ideal emotional climate in which to write.

CONTENTS

EXTRASENSORY PERCEPTION

APPENDIX

ABOUT THE AUTHOR

FOREWORD

*If I know nothing else, I know at least one thing is true:
that the sacred is in the ordinary, common things in life.*

– Bob Dylan
From the movie *Masked and Anonymous*

Though it is a common human experience, dreaming remains in the dark for most people. Even so, humankind has been attempting to explain, decipher, and pin down the meaning and purpose of dreams for centuries. Dozens of theories and techniques have evolved over the past few decades for exploring the mystery, yet the majority of people take—or perhaps have—little time to learn or utilize the techniques. This is a tragic cultural oversight.

Arthur Strock has rediscovered an ordinary way to amplify the value of dreams and allow individuals the opportunity to share meaningful dream experiences that otherwise would not have been disclosed. This way does not require long hours of study, participation in a dream group, or enlisting the services of a therapist. It is simply dream sharing.

In just ordinary conversation in everyday life, Arthur has developed the ability and intuition to seize the opportunity—when it presents itself—to encourage dialogue about dreams with family, friends and even complete strangers in conversations that may have begun with safe, popular subjects such as the weather. For example, in the stories, we see a muscular policeman transform into a tender-hearted grandson, recalling his beloved grandmother's assurance that she would always be with him. We experience a very bored father and his equally bored children at a Laundromat become enchanted with paper airplanes that Arthur has created. We take a visit to the barbershop and inadvertently Arthur assists one of the employees to achieve closure regarding her mother's death, and the assurance that her mother remains alive in another realm. We see a retired war veteran struggling with PTSD and cancer transformed into an excited young boy while recalling his favorite flying dreams. All are meaningful encounters borne of what began as ordinary exchanges with people in the course of everyday life.

Dr. Strock's experience and education regarding each of the encounters in the field of dreams is evident in the insight he imparts throughout the book. In the appendix, he has further categorized each encounter to enlighten the reader as to the type of dream each encounter represents, e.g., Problem Solving, Relationships, Fear and Trauma, Religion and Spirituality, Children.

By reading this book, we can all profit in ordinary conversations by learning to become more astute at using dreams to enliven what are often casual, sometimes meaningless conversations. What a remarkably special and unpretentious way to integrate dream sharing into our culture.

—Roberta Ossana
Former Publisher/Editor, Dream Network Journal

PREFACE

"Arthur, you've got to start remembering your dreams!" Jo Ann, a stranger and fellow attendee at a foot reflexology workshop, had a voice that carried with it the authority of an announcer at a large sporting event.

It didn't matter to her in the least that she hardly knew me or that I had remembered only two dreams in my entire life. "Don't worry Arthur, just put a pad and pencil next to your bed. Make sure you tell your unconscious that you're going to remember your dreams, write them down and do something with them." Little did I know that taking her advice thirty-five years ago would be the first step in the creation of this book.

Many dreams later, I began talking with strangers about dreams as an alternative to discussing the weather in order to beat the boredom of waiting in checkout lines. It was also my intention to share my enthusiasm for dreams. Those discussions provided information that was worth writing about. I later replaced casual conversation with requests for dreams that could be used in a book. A common pattern emerged. People first announced that their dreams were "weird." The unspoken message was that they weren't crazy even if their dreams were. Then they would add that their dreams were also "…short and didn't mean anything." By making that statement, they supported society's ongoing public denial that dreams have value. At the same time, they had expressed an inner knowing that their dreams do have value and that they wanted to be told what those dreams meant.

The resulting dream discussions became opportunities for people to share their stories, in which dreams were just a part. People wished almost desperately to share those stories that opened a path to self-acceptance and self-understanding, stories that were in danger of being lost in the disconnect that occurs when sharing through texting and email.

The book was well underway as a collection of dreams that would illustrate dream interpretation techniques. The book's focus, however, went through a major change as a result of feedback regarding my presentation at an annual conference for the International Association for the Study of Dreams. People over the course of the several-day conference spoke about how much they appreciated the stories. Before leaving the conference, the book had changed from a book on dream interpretation to a collection of stories that provided their own interpretations.

Please enjoy these stories. They can be read silently or aloud to yourself and others. Retell the stories and allow your own wisdom to show through in the telling. Watch as they provide you with bits of insight regarding your own dreams and how to improve your life. With increased attention paid to dreams, you can expect increased dream recall and ease of understanding. Allow your dreams to take flight and in doing so allow your life to take flight and be the equal of any daydream you've ever had.

PROBLEM SOLVING

Beginner's Luck

Arthur Strock, Ph.D.

BEGINNER'S LUCK

Our first house was absolutely wonderful. And what a pleasure it was for my wife and me to sit poolside. Making it extra special was the colorful and fragrant flower garden complete with its tall, proud zinnias in full view on the opposite side of the pool. The jokes from friends about swimming pools cracking, tilting, and sliding downhill were far from my mind.

But the summer ended and with it, the zinnias. As they withered, they revealed a rotten insect-eaten board that was no longer keeping soil behind the garden in place. It had slipped partially down the hill behind the pool, revealing an ominous patch of sand. I began to walk on the slope, at times finding it difficult to get a foothold. The beautiful lush green ivy ground cover was hardly up to the task of holding the sand in place. Those old pool jokes revived themselves and were a good motivator for checking with a pool service to see if there was a potential problem. The test turned out to be a simple act of jamming a broom handle into the ground behind the pool to see how far down it would go. The pool man was shocked to see it sink a foot-and-a-half down. "You better get a retaining wall fast!"

After many inquiries, a contractor was finally located who said he could do the job. Once onsite, he unloaded a truck full of railroad ties and carefully set the bottom tier in place. Several hours later, he and his helper were carrying all of the railroad ties back up the hill and loading them on his truck.

"Hey, where ya going?" I asked. His answer broke through some indistinct muttering.

"Can't be done, the ties keep slipping out from under themselves." I called another contractor. He suggested using a couple of large preformed concrete retaining structures left over from an industrial job, but he couldn't figure out how to get them into the backyard. A third contractor suggested building a sixteen-foot high stone wall next to the hill. The idea seemed far-fetched and carried with it an astronomical price tag.

At the same time I was dealing with the retaining wall problem, I was taking a course on mind control that was guaranteed to be life changing. On the way to class, while trying to remember what the night's topic would be, a bright red, eye-catching convertible sports car zipped past me. The vanity license plate sent a clear message: DREAMS.

That night our assignment was to follow a set of instructions to program or initiate a dream that would solve a problem. My dream was to answer the question of how to get a retaining wall built. I woke up to inner music, *Waiting for the Robert E. Lee.* As I wrote down the title, I wondered what under the sun that old song had to do with my problem. Once I began writing, an entire dream presented itself.

I am standing in a large gymnasium, looking at the wall. Sitting at the top of the wall is Maynard Ferguson's Band portrayed by poker-playing dogs, including an English bulldog. One of the dogs is playing a trombone with its slide fully extended. In front of me, widely spaced are several of my colleagues from work standing perfectly erect facing the wall.

It was difficult to know where to start with an interpretation, so out came the local phone book. I hoped that someone named Robert E. Lee might be listed as a wall builder. No luck, but Robert Lee and his boat marina were listed. I gave him a call.

"Hi, my name's Arthur Strock. I was wondering, because you have a marina, if you could give me some information about retaining walls." He said no, that all he had built were a couple of little walls near the lake. Wanting to follow the dream, I took a trip up to the marina to see if I could get ideas by looking at his walls. No luck; didn't even see any walls.

My wife suggested calling her brother Jim, an engineer with the Army Corps of Engineers. "Hello Jim, how are ya doin? We need your help…" The problem was described without reference to the dream.

His response was quick, "Sure, be glad to help, but you'll have to wait. I'm overseeing the construction of the new locks on the Mississippi River." His word "wait" brought to life that dream phrase, "Waiting for the Robert E. Lee." Thinking there might be a connection between the Robert E. Lee and the Mississippi River, a little research revealed that the Robert E. Lee had been a steamboat on the Mississippi River.

A couple of weeks later, Jim caught a flight to New Jersey, and within a day he had confirmed that the hill had begun to slide and had designed a wall to solve the problem. His three-tier, railroad-tie wall had a deep footing to stabilize the hill and keep the swimming pool in place. In describing the wall, he finished up with an afterthought.

"We'll put in verticals, extra ties in front of the bottom tier, to make sure the wall stays in place." Explaining to Jim that I hadn't been able to find a contractor, he did a quick search and with one call found the ideal contractor who completed the job quickly and successfully.

Just being able to get an answer to a problem on the first try at programming a dream appears to be a case of beginner's luck. In this case, however, it was much more. Over the years, the dream has revealed itself as a powerful lesson in dreamwork. The dream beautifully illustrates the importance of looking for more than just simple symbolic meanings. Dreamwork is a creative process that involves the interplay of intuition and logical thought followed by action. If the action taken leads to a dead end, such as my naive and amusing attempt to find a wall builder named Robert E. Lee, it's time to change direction.

The dream also illustrated how to search for clues to dream interpretation. Plays on words, even with people's names, can be important. The gym wall in the dream became Jim's wall in waking life. People can represent things other than people. My coworkers standing so straight in the dream were transformed into the verticals of the wall. Even small details in dreams can be critical and often contain hidden information. The trombone's slide going out over the wall was confirmation in engineering terms that my pool could slide. The fact that one of the poker-playing dogs was English referenced my English mother who later insisted that she help pay for the wall. The reference to my mother was confirmed later when I came across the name of a recording by Maynard Ferguson and his band that featured his trombone playing. It was entitled *The Conquistador*, the name of my parents' condominium.

In addition, that first programmed dream was an introduction to the role music would play in my future dreams. Music has continued to be a source of significant dream information. That dream also led to dream sharing that paid additional unexpected dividends. While telling my mother about the dream, she released a family secret that my grandfather had dreamt true and had premonitions of what was to come in the lives of his friends and neighbors.

Yes, that first initiated dream can be thought of as a bit of beginner's luck, but it was so much more—a far-reaching inspirational introduction to the world of dreams.

NO WAY OUT

Maddie, one of my favorite teaching colleagues from years ago, would invite me into her home economics classes. We would teach the kids how to initiate dreams to see what it was like to be in different jobs.

"Hi Art, it's good to see you dear." Her eyes squinted behind thicker lenses than I remembered. A hug didn't interrupt the continuous flow of words. "Hey, I need advice. Should I retire? I don't know how to do it."

My head spun for a second. "Hi Maddie, why not just go to the personnel office?"

"No, I can't do that. I need my health benefits and I'm not old enough to get Medicare. I have to keep quiet until I get more surgery. I've got all these new parts, a new hip, a new knee, screws in my ankle—now I need my other knee done and Joe's not working."

"Maddie, couldn't you get disability?"

"No, I tried that for my hearing. It didn't work even though I'm deaf in spite of my hearing aids. The room heaters are so loud, I can't even hear the kids and the principal keeps writing me up for not listening to them. I can't hear them. And my mother is ninety-four; her sister lived to be a hundred and thirteen.

"My mother can't live on her own anymore; she's going blind, can't drive, and tells me it's no problem—she hitchhikes. I set up my house as a mother-daughter suite, but she doesn't want to move; says I'm too rural. She's scared of the bears near my house.

"So, what are you doing?"

After a quarter-of-an-hour's worth of hearing how Maddie's life had become an ongoing catastrophe, I needed a minute to recover. "I'm gathering dreams from people and writing a book of stories about them. I bet you remember how we used to get the kids dreaming about their lives and how they could solve some of their problems. Maybe you could solve some of your problems by using dreams."

Maddie's face had lost some of its tension. "Art, I'm so glad I saw you." Her old engaging smile had reappeared and was covering some of her pain. "I guess I just needed to get stuff off my chest, and it was good for me to talk to you again. The smile was becoming a bit mischievous. "I did have a dream the other night where my Mom was telling me how happy she was because my dad who is long gone came into her bedroom and they had really good sex. Maybe there's a lesson for me in that dream." Some of the old twinkle had returned to Maddie's eyes.

Like Maddie, we all want solutions to our everyday problems. And we want the solutions to come quickly so we can be free of the tiring mind prattle that goes along with trying to solve the problems. "What did I do to deserve this? It isn't fair. What am I supposed to do? Just tell me what to do and I'll do it. I don't have time for this!" In our exasperation at not knowing how to bring closure to our problems, we can look to our dreams for something concrete and tangible to do.

Maddie recalled a recent dream; she didn't find what she was looking for, but did find something even more valuable: help in dealing with how she could approach her problems. She found humor in the dream that provided some relief from the emotional pain that had immobilized her. The dream was a reminder for all of us that we are free to choose how we approach our problems. As Maddie utilizes her old sense of humor and lightheartedness, she will find that she has more energy to deal with even her most severe problems.

A MADE-UP DREAM

Friday night brought Susan and me to our usual booth at the local Chinese restaurant. Even before we were seated next to each other, a little head came into view from the booth behind us. The almost-four-year-old boy watched us intently as he listened to what we were saying.

Having just read the beginning of a child's storybook about knights and castles that I'd recently bought for my grandson, I welcomed him by sharing the story as far as I had read. Coming to a stopping place, in true picture book fashion, I took on the role of a white-haired old wizard and popped a question to the little hero. "So, what was your latest dream?" As he gravely thought about how to answer, I filled in the empty space by telling him my latest dream. "I dreamt about a rope and some cubes this morning." That was all that the little boy needed to hear. He immediately began telling me his rope dream.

I was shooting at these things as I was sliding down the rope with my bow and arrows.

"Now that's a neat dream; be sure to tell your mom about it." He scrambled to the other side of the booth to cuddle with his mom while he told her his increasingly elaborate dream.

His mother who had been smiling with interest over his discussion with me was now settling in to hear a very long dream.

Four-year-olds are known for being expansive. And true to form, when this little boy heard my dream, he fabricated his own right on the spot. Because children are young and innocent, we need to enjoy their fantasy, something that sometimes means setting aside our own need to be realistic and avoid such comments as "Are you sure that was your dream?" or "That's sweet, but I know you're just making it up." There's no doubt that the boy borrowed bits and pieces from the storybook as well as my dream, but that didn't matter.

Unknowingly, he had provided his mom with an important relationship building opportunity. If she continues to be a good listener, and it would be difficult not to be with such an exuberant, charming little boy, she will further deepen her relationship with him. She can encourage dream sharing by telling him some of her own dreams, edited of course.

Adults often have a concern that fostering a child's imagination may encourage immaturity. Just the opposite occurs. Dreamwork helps develop the insight of right brain activity and provides a healthy balance to the logic of left brain activity so heavily emphasized in the school setting. Dream sharing with children is an effortless creative activity where the child can strengthen his or her own sense of self worth. In addition, dream sharing with children has the unexpected and added benefit of stimulating adult intuition as well.

I'll need to finish reading the story about the princes and their castles so I can tell the little boy what happens if I see him again at the restaurant. There is a chance though that he will take my story to bed with him and finish it in his own dreams, then have something to tell me.

HOUSE-BUYING WORRIES

The phone rang. "I've gotta tell ya a dream." The words were jammed together and came from a high-pitched voice. It was panic—Shannon didn't even begin with the usual "Hi Dad." She didn't wait for my response either. Out toppled the dream.

Eric and I are buying this house—a sixty-year-old monster-large house; the master bedroom is the size of our living room and dining room combined. It was all filthy. We walked through and every part of the house was in shambles and needed something done to it. I opened closets and life-sized puppets started out on a track at me, but got stuck. Eric said no problem; he could oil them. The bathroom was all broken apart and was covered by a sheet of something and would take six thousand dollars to repair and put back together. The backyard was just as bad. The pool was scummy and disgusting and the kids next door were always using it and I had to tell them that they would have to make arrangements in advance because my children would be using it.

"I woke up fast and right away started to worry. You know we're buying a house that Eric and I both love. I thought I was dreaming about our new house. What were we going to do? Was the house going to turn into a nightmare? So I took a deep breath to calm myself and the thought came to mind that Eric and I were safe. What a relief. The house in the dream was one we almost bought two years ago. I'm so glad we didn't get that one. The house was old, much bigger than we needed and was way over budget. We would have been in big trouble. I went back and checked my notes. I had written that we could not afford anything over $280,000. That house was $350,000. With the higher payments we'd be broke now. Guess how much the house we're buying costs? House plus fees takes us to $280,000. I am so relieved. You know, it must have been all that pizza I ate just before going to bed."

Shannon nailed it. Not just because she's my daughter. It's no old wives' tale that eating just before going to bed can cause nightmares, just as some medications can. In this case, the combination of heightened anxiety around an ongoing life event and eating the pizza triggered the nightmare.

I knew that Shannon had been worried about the purchase of a house. Her worries had turned into "what if" thinking which usually leads to thinking of disasters. And house buying more often than not does not go according to plan. When we experience heightened emotion during the day, the dream will deal with it. The emotion we feel most often becomes the central emotion of the dream. In this case, Shannon's extreme anxiety was not appropriate to the house that she and her husband were buying. Buying a house, however, had revived feelings of vulnerability that Shannon had felt previously. Much to the dismay of dreamers, dreams such as Shannon's are normal. Fear and anxiety are the most common emotions experienced in dreams.

SUPERMARKET DELI COUNTER

Custom-made sandwiches at the Foodtown deli department were the best bargain in town. I was looking forward to a super sandwich with all the extras.

There was only one customer ahead of me. He was kidding with the guy behind the counter who was making my sandwich, a friend with a history of being late to work. The customer lost little time, drawing me into the conversation by turning to me and saying, "It's good to be on time, right?" His overwhelming size made it easy to nod my head in agreement. Even at a glance, the contrast between the two of us was striking. He was a tall, talkative, large-framed, and very dark-skinned African American. I'm a short, quiet, small-framed, thin, and very light-skinned European American. The man proved to be more than just a good talker; he was a very good listener and listened carefully as the woman making his sandwich told him her sad story. She handed him the sandwich but he waited patiently until she was finished talking. By that time, my sandwich was ready too.

The man was ready to go. A dynamic person who can listen as well as talk is rare and suggests a level of insight that is so valuable for working with dreams. I wondered what kind of dreams he had. Because he had already turned to go, I knew I didn't have much time as I blurted out my request. "I'm writing a book about dreams and wondered if you would tell me one of yours. " His friendly look turned menacing, "I don't dream." He looked to the side. "I mean, I don't remember them." The guy drooped as we continued walking to the front cash registers. "I just get bad ones." His paced quickened. "They're all the same, just like my life. I'm out of a job; I fill out the applications and I go for interviews. They ask about the trouble I got into. I tell them and then I don't get hired."

Tentatively I asked if there wasn't something he could do to change the scenario, possibly talking to HR ahead of time. He assured me that there was nothing he could do, going on to emphasize the point with an explanation about the poor economy.

By this time, we'd gotten through the checkout and were out of the supermarket. He was hurrying away toward a waiting car that was obviously his ride. Wanting to do something to help, I shouted a recommendation that just before going to sleep, he redo the dream as he would want it to turn out. The comment stopped him in his tracks.

He called back, "You mean a *good* dream?"

"Yes! Give your unconscious a powerful message about what you want; maybe you'll get some new ideas about how to get a job."

He went into slow-motion mode as he reached for the car door and said half to himself, "I'll do it." As he got into the car, he reached out to me with his arm above the door window, "You come here much?"

"Yeah, on Thursdays; let me know what happens."

The market closed unexpectedly and I never did get to find out what happened. He responded so positively that it seemed he already had an understanding that we affect our dreams by what we focus on during the day. My recommendations were accepted so quickly, he may well have had similar recommendations previously, mine just being a confirmation of what he already knew or had been told.

The incident, however, was far more than just a five-minute dream discussion. The experience proved how powerful dream sharing can be as a way to break through the potential barriers of age, race, socioeconomic status, and even physical size.

I hope our conversation gave him the will to persevere. Job-hunting is difficult enough without some of the adversities that he is facing. I also hope he reads this book. If he does, I hope he'll contact me and let me know how the new dream worked out.

Arthur Strock, Ph.D.

PERSONAL STYLE

A Bad Hair Day

A BAD HAIR DAY

It was looking like rain as I stopped at the Valley Fruit Farm stand to get some of the sweetest, juiciest, and best-tasting peaches ever. As I filled my bag, a large SUV pulled up.

A sprightly looking woman hopped out of the cab and in a loud voice called, "So, how's retirement treating you Dr. Strock?" She didn't look familiar but must have recognized me from my days working in the local school system.

"Things are going well. I enjoy sleeping late, have more time for writing, and more time to chat with people and collect dreams for my book. Want to share a dream?"

"As a matter of fact, I do. I had a bizarre dream a few days ago and I wish I knew what it meant."

The lady I'll refer to as Jenny took me aside to the edge of the display stand area. She was in such a hurry to find out what the dream meant, she was out of breath by the time she finished.

Julie, my best friend, next-door neighbor, dropped by just to visit. She said she didn't like the color of my hair and asked if she could change it. I liked my hair color, but she kept on me about it. When I asked her what she knew about hair coloring and how long it would take, she said she'd never done it and knew absolutely nothing about hair coloring. But she was so insistent, I finally just said "yes." She got to work but was taking forever. My hair was beginning to look really gross. Then it started falling out! I panicked right on the spot and woke up crying.

"What's it mean?"

Most people like the idea of a quick symbolic interpretation. So I was tempted to tell her the generic meanings for things in her dream. For example, color often represents the mood of the dreamer. Hair can represent the dreamer's thoughts, while a friend can represent a distinguishing feature of the dreamer. Fortunately I didn't bring up such meanings because they can be misleading and Jenny had already begun exploring the context of the dream.

"I don't get it; the hair thing shouldn't be a big deal. When my friends are upset about their hair, I always make them feel better by telling them not to worry, 'If you have a bad hair day, it'll grow back.'" She then stopped talking and was obviously stuck. I asked her what had been on her mind before having the dream. She drew a blank.

It was time for a different approach. "Jenny, do this. Imagine you're back at the beginning of the dream and replay it as a good dream this time."

Okay. My best friend from next door drops by to say hello. She looks at my hair and tells me how it would look even nicer if it was a different color and that she had a lot of experience using hair colorings. After thinking about it, I tell her that I'll honor her opinion and let her do it. It doesn't take long to do my hair and I like the new color.

The dream replay generated a deep insight for Jenny. She lit up. "I got it. It's about processing what people are asking me to do. You see, I'm a people pleaser, especially with my friends, and I usually say yes even before giving it a thought. I don't like to say no. I want to be able to say yes, but not because they're pushing me."

Jenny's use of the word processing turned out to be the key to developing a strategy for dealing with people in waking life who ask her to do things she doesn't want to do. I suggested that she tell people, "I need to process that." She said that it seemed logical and she might as well give it a try. I gave her a guarantee that she would get a chance to try her new strategy. I also asked her to let me know what happened when she used it.

There was no need to wait. As Jenny headed over to the bins of fruit, a clerk who had been lingering near us meandered over to Jenny under the pretense of straightening out some of the fruit displays. Their conversation was just barely audible.

The sales clerk asked Jenny if she had gotten an interpretation for her dream, revealing how interested she herself was in dreams. Jenny avoided the question with a comment about her friend being a psychologist, but the clerk persisted saying that she'd love to hear his thoughts. Jenny mumbled that she'd forgotten already.

Not taking no for an answer the clerk blurted out, "What did it mean?"

Jenny froze, avoided eye contact, and looking trapped, put out her hand as if to say "no" and in a way that seemed completely out of character, she mumbled, "I need to process it."

The clerk gave up. Before Jenny left, I caught up with her and as we talked, she confided in me she hadn't realized that she had been asked to tell the meaning of the dream three separate times. She explained that in such situations her mind always went blank and was shut down to anything other than saying "yes." Jenny said that in the future she was going to be more alert to situations where people insisted that she do something.

It had begun to drizzle. The effect on Jenny's hair was a quick frizz. Anybody looking at her would have thought she was having a really bad hair day. But as she moved back to her SUV, her perkiness returned. After a lifetime of struggle in dealing with unwanted requests, Jenny had made a breakthrough. She had come up with a way of at least postponing an answer that wouldn't hurt anyone's feelings. She's now in a position to take the final step, developing a way to simply say no when she wants to say no.

Once in the driver's seat, she began laughing. Her eyes sparkled as she lowered the window. "I can't wait to tell my neighbor what happened—all because of a dream."

A DOCTOR'S DREAMS

I didn't like the idea of having such a big long needle pushed into my neck. It didn't seem to make sense just to get a tiny sample of the thyroid tissue for the biopsy.

The nurse had been very pleasant, quite amiable in the way she described the process. "You'll get an injection of a local anesthetic. When the biopsy needle goes in, you'll feel some pressure on your neck followed by two or three mild bang-like sounds—like a cap gun going off; that's when the end of the needle closes and cuts out the samples."

The doctor was younger than expected and seemed modestly unassuming with just a hint of what might in later years become a slight stoop in posture. His entire being gave a message of transparency and understated confidence. His expression was focused and clear of distractions as he maintained relaxed but direct and honest-looking eye contact.

Dr. Richardson worked easily with both the nurse and the X-ray technician in locating the thyroid area he would be sampling. He also provided an appreciated commentary as he went through each step of the biopsy process and unexpectedly finished with the words, "All done." I asked why there hadn't been a third "banging" sound. He explained that the procedure went smoothly and he had gotten exactly what was needed.

As he began putting his instruments away, I mentioned that my specialty was dreams, and that I wondered if he dreamed about his work. His head tilted slightly upward, his features softening even more as he considered my question thoughtfully. He continued to be unhurried as the other two medical people looked up at him in silence. He then turned to me and with just a hint of self consciousness, explained that he was considered to be an expert in doing problematic biopsies and that his work was sometimes made more difficult when his assistants were nervous.

At that point, the nurse and technician couldn't contain themselves any longer and excitedly began talking about difficult patients and how some of them would kick and scream for even minor procedures and needed to be held down in order to prevent injuries. It was clear that the nurse and technician would have enjoyed talking more about their most difficult cases. In his reserved manner, however, the doctor stopped them by completing his answer to my question, saying that when his staff members were upset, he would have dreams that night. He quietly returned to putting away his instruments. His assistants returned to telling their tales.

Dr. Richardson had answered my question. His response was direct while at the same time being a soft-spoken request for privacy and a gentle indication that he had completed his contribution to the conversation.

Dr. Richardson's natural, quiet, and modest air of self-confidence attested to his competency. Nevertheless, his thoughtful and conscientious style suggested that the dreams he had referred to could be performance-related dreams. Performance dreams are prompted by feelings of being tested in waking life. In a sense, every procedure a doctor performs is at least partially a test of his ability. Procedures done during the day may go unnoticed by one's dreams if they go well and engender no strong emotional reactions. Because Dr. Richardson is a sensitive individual, even if he was initially satisfied with his performance, the nervousness of attending staff could raise unconscious or possibly conscious questions of his performance. His dreams could deal with any unresolved issues in order to provide a learning experience of knowing what could have gone wrong.

Performance dreams often include school experiences with good or bad test scores, adequate or poor preparation, and strong feelings of success or failure. Most people have more dreams of poor performance than good performance, but I would hope that Dr. Richardson's dreams recognize his good work and give him top grades.

Arthur Strock, Ph.D.

WHO'S CUTTING WHO OFF?

It was the fifty-fifth high school class reunion dinner. There she was, Lanie Mitchell. Sixty years before, I had chased her around our seventh-grade classroom, encouraged by all her laughing and giggling. Our teacher, Mr. Callum—tall, good-looking, idolized, and just out of the military—stopped us instantly with his no-nonsense tone of voice. We were to return to our seats and stay after school. In those days, staying after school was serious business.

Now sixty years later, not having had any interactions with Lanie since graduation, I moved to her table and spoke of the incident, which she had totally forgotten. The story seemed to tickle her along with everyone else at the table, but we quickly moved on to more recent events and interests including my interest in dreams. Lanie shared a dream that she had that afternoon during a nap before the dinner.

It was a very short dream. A car cut me off and it woke me up.

Lanie interpreted the dream with little emotion, explaining that she had felt cut off from other kids at school. And with an air of socially acceptable conviction, added that now that she was older, "It really didn't matter." The other people at the table were quick to agree and support her interpretation.

How often have we heard that old shallow reassurance that it really didn't matter? It comes in different guises: "Oh just forget it: let it rest; get on with your life; it really wasn't important."

Nevertheless, the undeniably painful feelings of being cut off from others do matter and can be expected to break through to the surface until they are dealt with. More than a half-century later, Lanie's dream was a reminder of what it is like to be cut off. It's doubtful that the dream emerged just to reassure her that feeling cut off was of no consequence. It's more likely that the dream was waking her up to an unsettled issue.

Lanie's interpretation dealt with the feelings of being cut off as if they were just a natural consequence of living without any underlying reason. What had happened during her school years? Had her classmates cut her off? Had she cut herself off from them? Her dream suggests that she was actively involved. Dream characters most frequently represent the dreamer. In Lanie's dream, the driver was not identified, increasing the probability that she was the driver and was symbolically cutting herself off. Didn't she feel popular? Didn't she feel worthy of closer friendships?

Regardless of the reason, it is likely that at a deeper level Lanie still feels cut off from others. If so, the dream came with perfect timing. What better time to remedy such a problem than a reunion dinner? It was an excellent opportunity for her to step out of her comfort zone and approach those very people from whom she felt cut off. Even more importantly, in doing so she would be making a statement to herself and others that she is indeed someone who deserves to be accepted.

Wondering if Lanie had given the dream any more thought, I called her after the reunion and left a voice message. She replied with an email. "I will return your call when I'm not fixing supper, on my way out, or heading to read in bed. I don't want to call you at an inconvenient time." A couple of days later, she called and mentioned that she had been visiting with several members of our high school class when my call came in on her cell phone.

She added that she hadn't reconsidered the dream and didn't really believe in things like horoscopes.

Dreams are such an integral part of us that Lanie's active rejection of her dreams supports the idea that metaphorically she may be cutting herself off in some way. The only way to know would be if Lanie decided to share just how and when feelings of being rejected come to the surface. Hopefully, she will have decided to make friends with her dreams by the next reunion. If not, her dreams will be hard at work trying a new way to convey their message.

DR. REIKI

Clara was a dynamic, savvy social worker. She was also a skilled dreamer, who, knowing my interest in dreams, sent me an email about a dream that she found particularly exciting:

> So I got up this morning knowing I had an incredible dream, but I couldn't remember it. I hate it when that happens. So I went through my recall routine. First, I wrote down the question, "What did I dream?" Then I began writing whatever came to my mind for the next five or ten minutes. It didn't work. Next I wrote down, "Let go, let God, and wait. It'll come when it's ready." It didn't work.
>
> Finally as a last ditch effort before I started running with my day; I turned to meditation, planning just ten or fifteen minutes. Of course my mind was starting to speed up with what I needed to do during the day. I told myself, "Come back and focus. Mindfulness. Rise above."
>
> Yay, success! It didn't even take ten minutes. Here's the dream, Arthur:
>
> *Dr. R, whom I'll call Dr. Reiki, is giving me Reiki healing!*
> *I never dreamed of energetic healing before—not in any*

form that I can remember. Anyway, Dr. R has his hands over my right lower ribs. I feel the very warm healing energy on my side. It feels wonderful! In my dream he didn't appear to know that I was aware of his presence.

Interesting, because just yesterday I sought out yoga centers, some with certified Reiki masters, but the most important thing I've been focused on in recent weeks is whether or not my new boss is really going to support me. He is quiet and noncommunicative until he decides to come forward with his decisions. I think I got my answer. What do you think?

Clara got her answer in the knowing that Dr. Reiki represented her boss. With many concerns that can come with getting a new job, Clara was reassured that she does not have to be worried about her relationship with her boss. She interpreted the dream to mean that not only will he be nontoxic, but also that he can be relied upon to support her in a healing manner.

Clara's email was a reminder of the way in which many people get discouraged when their dreams fly from memory even before they get out of bed. As a result, they resign themselves to forgetting dreams, not realizing that perseverance can pay off by using strategies to enhance recall. Clara mentioned some strategies that work well for her and can work well for others too.

An additional strategy for catching that elusive dream can be used as a good first step. Try simply lying still and clearing the mind while having the effortless intention of allowing the dream to resurface. You may find that this technique turns out to be an example of how sometimes doing less is really doing more.

WAITING TO BE ASKED

It was very quiet at the dream conference bookstore. The only person there was the person tending the store, and she was miles away immersed in a book. The absence of people made it easy for me to make my selections. As I approached the checkout table, the woman raised her head and closed her book. Her offer of help was given with a slightly reserved smile and a warm, soft voice just hinting at her southern background. Her quiet, welcoming manner offered me an opening to suggest that one day she might be selling my book. The very gracious way she questioned me about my book prompted me to ask if she'd had any good dreams lately.

Evonne's reply was pure velvet covering just a hint of electricity. "Yes and I've been wanting to tell someone, but nobody's asked; it's just a short dream." After the slightest pause she continued. "I need to give you a little background information first. I have recurring dreams of my husband. He died twenty years ago and I usually get disturbed by the dreams. This morning I had one, but I wasn't disturbed at all."

I was kissing my husband with passionate feeling.

"I realized that if I could still feel passion like that, I was beginning to respect myself as an older woman. I don't need to hold on to the memory of my youth any longer and I can release the memory of my deceased husband." Evonne's direct but dreamy gaze left no doubt that her husband had received quite a kiss and maybe more.

"Sounds like a new you," I said.

"Oh yes, I've been the new me all day. I've been free to connect and be happy and interact with people openly. It's been a wonderful day. I haven't let any fears of being old interfere with being me."

Evonne now looked so genuinely attractive there was little doubt that her new vibrancy would find men turning their heads for a second look.

"I wouldn't be surprised if you start getting invited out for coffee or a drink." A hesitant response broke through a hint of anticipation.

"My, that would certainly be a next step."

Evonne's dream illustrates how dreams can chart personal development. Our dream behavior reflects our waking behavior. If we pay attention to behavior changes in dreams, we catch a glimpse of how we've changed in ways that are just on the cusp of conscious awareness.

The dream may have prompted Evonne to embrace the clarity of thinking that can come with maturity and allow her to release possible beliefs of not being good enough or not deserving happiness. The dream may have been in response to a need to love again. Another possibility is that Evonne may have gotten tired of taking a passive role in living her life. Looking ahead, she may also get tired of waiting for a man to ask her out. She may just take the bull by the horns and do the asking herself.

FAMILY

A Cry for Help

A CRY FOR HELP

Kora was bouncing with excitement as she completed preparing the order for my oil change. She was a dependable mainstay at the local garage and relished the opportunity to share dreams whenever my car needed attention.

"I want to tell you my dream—but first here's my situation. You know I'm a single parent, but I just gained custody of my cousin's little eight-month-old baby boy. It's a long story. Anyway, he sleeps in the bedroom with me and my ten-year-old daughter. Our bedroom is very, very noisy. Every night it's vroom, vroommm bummmp bump. The racket and rumble of trucks outside the window goes on all night long."

In my dream, I see a white pickup truck flying past my window. It looked like the tornado in The Wizard of Oz. *I wake up my daughter, grab the baby, and head for the basement. But, just as I start out of the bedroom, the door slams shut. I hear my daughter frantically crying out again and again, "Mommy, help me!" I fight with the door but can't get it open. I know the tornado is hitting the house now. I wonder, do I go and save the baby, or do I save my daughter? I never got a chance to make the decision. I woke up to that horrible bumping noise of trucks on the street outside.*

Kora, a lively talker and a good communicator, wanted to make sure I got the whole story of how she reacted to the dream. She said her daughter's cry for help in the dream seemed to be the same as a cry for help in real life. She woke up knowing that she'd been spending all her time with the baby and had neglected her daughter. When told about the dream her daughter pleaded, "You wouldn't have left me would you?"

Kora's smile was infectious. "I took my daughter with me for a manicure and a pedicure. It cost me almost $100!" Looking a bit impish, she apologized for being so extravagant. "It was a crazy dream."

Kora is a dreamworker par excellence. She moved beyond an illusory academic dream interpretation that would have unconsciously kept her from initiating needed life changes. Kora integrated her daughter's dream cry for help into her waking life and responded in the most loving and meaningful way she could imagine.

The dream had presented Kora with an either/or decision: save the baby or save her daughter. In waking life, Kora transcended the limitations of the dream. She made the decision that neither child was going to be sacrificed for the sake of the other.

The dream and its real life outcome is already on its way to becoming a family chronicle, reaffirming a mother's love for her two children. If kept alive with retelling, the story will take on new meanings for each of the family members. It should also provide the next generation with a strong incentive to continue the family's dreamwork tradition.

A BROKEN HEART

The presentation on autism was well attended. The twenty-eight-year-old speaker's appearance captured the group's attention. Julianne's long, beautiful, dark hair was riveting, but at odds with her large, almost bushy eyebrows that contributed to a pervasive look of unchanging melancholy. Her facial expression was emphasized by the downturn in the corners of her mouth that even an occasional attempted smile couldn't change. She openly told her bleak life story that included a diagnosis of autism early in life. Julianne's family description included a very quiet submissive mother from Columbia, a loud domineering Italian-American father from New York City, and a talented younger brother who upstaged her in all activities. Her presentation was filled with emotion and did much to dispel the outmoded stereotype of autistic individuals as being insensitive.

The topic of dreams was not brought up during the presentation. Because dreams are so personal, I chose to ask Julianne about her dreams in private following the presentation. Her expression changed slightly as she quietly considered the question of whether or not she used her dreams to deal with everyday problems. After careful consideration, she said that when she was younger, she heard the tune "Don't Go Breaking My Heart" again and again as she awoke. The music was not accompanied by any visual or story line component.

I asked if she had felt that her heart was being broken by someone back then. She struggled with the question and answered by saying that the Beatles was her favorite vocal group and their songs helped her feel that love could be real and not dishonest.

Words-only dreams, those in which the dreamer hears words spoken by an unidentified and unseen speaker, hold special significance. The words can represent truth, sometimes an ultimate truth for the dreamer. Words to music heard in dreams can also be a message of truth. The message can be considered even more important if repeated several times either on consecutive nights or spaced over time.

Julianne's recurring musical dream of "Don't Go Breaking My Heart" may also be considered as a words-only dream. It confirmed her emotional sensitivity and identified her as having a broken heart before she was fully aware of it. Her comment about how she experienced love at the time suggests that not only was she brokenhearted, but that others were being deceptive regarding their feelings for her.

How was Julianne's heart broken and who broke it? It would be easy to point the finger at any one of her family members, because her family members undoubtedly showed their love in very different ways. To do so we would simply be falling into the trap of thinking we know better than the dreamer how to draw conclusions from a dream. If she were interested in sharing more information, there are more questions that could be asked, starting with questions about her family relationships. Perhaps such questions would plant seeds of thought that could grow into a mature understanding of the reason for the dream.

Because she recalled her old recurring theme so quickly, the issue of being loved is clearly still relevant. Julianne's thoughts and realizations about how her heart was broken might be surprising. What might surprise us even more would be to see the corners of her mouth tilt up and allow her to have a true heartfelt smile, the kind we give when our hearts have been mended.

GRANDPARENTS

End of season at the Van Heusen outlet stores is the best time for getting bargains at 80 and 85 percent off retail prices. The new sales clerk was playfully effervescent.

"You should really buy this shirt." The shirt was a leftover with a tropical pattern that hadn't been in style for longer than I could remember.

"But why should I buy it?"

Her silly smile said it all, "Because it's the last one."

Having just come from my office, dreams were still on my mind and I got to wondering if the salesgirl was a dreamer.

"I'm writing a book on dreams and I was wondering if you could help me out with a dream."

Her face became earnest, "I never dream."

"But I do." The partially muffled voice came from behind a clothing rack as a head popped up. Then the rest of her popped up. Gloria was carrying a load of blouses on hangers. "I dream all the time, you should hear this one.

"You see, the day before my dream, I was going to visit my aunt and passed the turnoff for getting to my grandparents' house. I loved them very much. I remembered years of wonderful visits. I really missed them and wished that I could visit them again. We lived next door for the first nine years of my life and I spent most of my time with them in their kitchen because my parents were never home. But they died a few years ago. The morning after I'd been doing all this thinking about them, I had a dream of visiting them in their kitchen. Now, I've dreamt about being in the kitchen with my grandmother before, but this time even my grandfather was there."

Everything was excruciatingly clear and exactly the way it was before they died: clothes that needed repair hanging by the door, the sewing machine in the corner, the refrigerator next to the old kitchen table and chairs, the old radio on the shelf, even my grandfather's false teeth next to the sink. And my grandmother was sitting there smiling and listening to me. We talked and talked. And my grandfather—he was quiet as usual, but looked so good, just the way he looked before he got sick. Suddenly my grandmother stood up and said, "It's time to go now."

"Just then, my alarm went off. It was time to get ready for work. But during my real visits when I was a kid my grandmother never told me to go. This dream made feel like I wasn't wanted."

Dreams frequently fulfill our wishes. Gloria's wish to see her grandparents again certainly came true. She felt so happy to see her grandparents, but also felt sad, wondering if her grandmother didn't really love her anymore. Gloria probably didn't consider how grandparents and parents never lose their love or the sense of responsibility for their children's welfare. Her grandmother's comment most likely came not out of any loss of love, but out of the love she had for Gloria as a child, not wanting her to get in trouble for being late.

The dream is important in how it draws our attention to time in additional ways. It not only came immediately after Gloria's wish to see her grandparents, but it lets us know that those on the other side of the veil are aware of time on this plane.

Gloria's description of the dream as being "excruciatingly clear" gives us the clue that the dream was very special in another way. Dreams that have a sharper-than-Blu-ray quality often have a spiritual component. Gloria's dream is an example of a visitation that goes beyond a spoken reassurance by the deceased that he or she is okay. Gloria learned that her deceased grandfather was more than just okay; he was healthy again. Gloria's dream was a bittersweet reminder of the undying love of grandparents. If we thank them for their love, they'll hear us.

ALEX SWALLOWED A PENNY

A call from my daughter Shannon continued our long tradition of dream sharing. "Dad, Alex swallowed a penny. I read a lot of advice on the internet about what to do if your child swallows a coin. I learned about danger signs. The newer pennies can cause chemical reactions if they get lodged in there somewhere because they're more than just copper. I knew it wasn't lodged in his throat. He didn't show any signs of breathing trouble, and he didn't have a tummy ache. Recommendations were so different. Some sites recommended an immediate trip to the emergency room. One site said there should be no problem unless the coin doesn't come out in three or four weeks. I decided to follow advice suggesting a trip to the doctor if it didn't come out in seven days. That night I had a dream."

I was all over the place and saw a male doctor on day number seven who said I didn't need to do anything for seventy-eight days.

"I interpreted the dream to mean that I did not have to worry unless the penny stayed in for more than seven or eight days. So I checked all of Alex's poop—that was two or three times a day. On day number five, there it was. I don't know what happened to it in there because it had turned a weird black color, so I scrubbed it and saved it as a souvenir. Later in retrospect, I think the dream was just telling me to chill out."

People often don't appreciate the connection between dream information and the physical body. That connection can carry over from a child to a mother, more likely if the mother is an experienced dreamer.

If the swallowed coin was becoming a problem, Shannon would most likely have received a dream warning similar to ones she had received in the past; she is an experienced dreamer. Grampy might have been a bit more concerned than his daughter. But other than remembering that his best friend in grammar school swallowed a quarter, Grampy had no experience with coin swallowing. His daughter was the perfect little girl who never did swallow a coin.

Not long after Shannon told me about Alex, I brought up the topic of children swallowing coins at a community picnic. A neighbor spoke of her son Jerry who had never swallowed a coin, but at age four put a pebble in his ear. He told his mom how he tried to get it out but couldn't. Looking into his ear, his mom didn't see any sign of a pebble, but Jerry insisted that it was there. The pediatrician couldn't see the pebble either, so they went to an ear, nose, and throat specialist. The entire situation began to take on a Dr. Seuss-like quality as the doctors and nurses examined Jerry's ear.

Jerry never did think his mother believed him. If his mother had recalled her dreams at the time, a dream might have given her the proof she was looking for. We can only imagine how her dreams could have alerted her to the presence of the pebble. She might have seen the Rock of Gibraltar in his ear; she might have been kissing the Blarney Stone, unearthing the Rosetta Stone, or even heard the tune "A Rolling Stone Gathers no Moss." The possibilities are endless.

Jerry had to wait thirty-seven years to prove himself and have the last laugh. While working out one day, he heard the echo of the pebble moving in his ear, not the first time he had heard the sound. But this time, he cupped his hand over his ear, leaned to the side and shook his head vigorously. What he believed to be the long-lost pebble dropped out. It now sits on a miniature velvet cushion, proudly displayed on his Facebook page. Thank goodness Alex didn't have to wait thirty-seven years.

DAD, WHERE ARE YOU?

My daughter Shannon was the cutest, dearest little girl. As a preschooler, she would run and play with her thumb stuck in her mouth, her long, curly blond hair moving in every direction, and her ever-present blankie trailing along behind.

It was during those early years that our dream sharing began. As she got older, our relationship grew during our trips in a home-built plywood canoe. She sat in the bow, sometimes using her little paddle, sometimes holding the field glasses to her eyes taking on the responsibilities of a lookout. Sledding took the place of canoeing during the winter, but whatever we did, we had wonderful adventures together.

Our relationship survived her teenage years and a marital breakup that resulted in a new and deeper fondness for each other. Our annual trip for a Christmas show in New York City is a happily anticipated tradition we hope will continue for another twenty years. Over time, my little girl's sweet innocence has grown into a spiritually based integrity that has added to the value of our times together and our long phone calls.

We took advantage of the phone company's family plan and have used our cell phones to shrink the distance between us following Shannon's out-of-state job change and subsequent marriage. Still later, Shannon called to share dreams during her pregnancy. Without realizing it, our phone calls and dream sharing became less frequent following the excited flurry of calls around the birth of little Annabelle.

One morning my voice mail included a desperate-sounding call. "Dad, I had a dream last night that was really sad—I need to share it." I made a quick return call and heard the dream.

I was traveling back and forth in different times and dimensions. I was trying to reach you. It was so real!

A group of us was trying to get a big old school bus to cross dimensions. Just as it was about ready, another group came out of hiding and interfered with the bus trip to your dimension. The dream evaporated.

Then, I tried to reach you by cell phone. You were in a different time period. You had a cell phone, but because you were living in the 1800s it was impossible for you to charge the battery. I was frightened that I might never talk to you again.

Considering the meaning of the dream, it could be said that metaphorically it was Annabelle who came out of hiding. Being Annabelle's mother, Shannon was taking time that previously had been spent being my daughter. Shannon was struggling with what it was like to be in the dual role of mother and daughter. During our conversation, Shannon said that she realized how her daughter was a member of the new generation, a frightening realization because it meant that her dad was a member of the older generation and that I wouldn't be around forever. She said she missed me and wanted to soak up as much of me as possible before I was gone.

Although I'm still very much alive, the dream placed me in the 1800s, a bit behind the times. So the dream had a message for me too. I needed to keep up with the times and follow modern cell phone etiquette—make sure the cell phone is left on, check for missed calls, and charge the battery.

Now that my cell phone is on, Shannon is able to cross into my dimension. We're once again enjoying each other's company as valued confidants. And there's an added benefit; Grandpa gets to connect with that beautiful little baby Annabelle.

CHILDREN

At the Laundromat

AT THE LAUNDROMAT

The heavy Laundromat door was tough to squeeze through with an overloaded basket of laundry, hangers and detergent. Once through, the scene was familiar: people busy at washers and dryers in the front, some empty machines in the back. But this time there was a scene within a scene, seemingly separated from the Laundromat itself.

A young father was sitting in a chair looking listlessly over the aisle at the TV while his three children stood lifeless next to him. The six-year-old boy was motionless almost invisible in front of the dryers. Standing close to his side was a thin, woebegone-looking little girl with long, almost-blond, tangled hair and shapeless clothing. The cover of her tightly held Disney storybook showed Princes Ariel dressed in a gorgeous pink gown, a picture that could not match the winning beauty of the little girl's sad lonely face. The youngest, not yet four, was leaning against her. The children were past the point of protest, resigned to the boredom of mindless waiting until their laundry was finished.

Although the image of the family caught my eye, it dissolved with my need to find empty washers. Then, back to the front of the store again to get change for the machines. The coin changer sucked in the bill and began clanking out the quarters like a Vegas one-armed bandit, giving a false impression that I had just won the jackpot. And just like in Vegas, no one seemed interested.

I threw a glance at the kids. They were still there, but just as before, they made no movement.

After my winnings had been lost to the washers, I noticed an unread Avon catalog—no creases, no torn edges, perfect paper-airplane material. Why not? Those kids looking like they were at a funeral needed relief. Actually, plenty of reasons why not: a complete stranger in a Laundromat approaching little kids could seem pretty suspicious even if they were standing next to their father. My legs were taking me toward the kids before my mind had the sense to stop me. An empty table next to the kids provided a perfect place to fold. It was also between the children and me, providing the father with a barrier of safety for the children if he felt it was needed.

Looking down at the table, I took a chance, "Paper airplanes?" The father didn't respond, but didn't object either. The children just stood there, but their heads seemed to turn just a little bit in my direction. I made the first couple of folds.

With a glance toward the kids, I said, "Look at this: what's it look like now?" No answer. With exaggerated enthusiasm, my words came out a little louder than expected, "A house, doesn't it?" Still no response, but at least the kids no longer looked dead. Next fold, "Now what's it look like?" Desperate, I called out, "An envelope, right?"

The little girl came alive and called out, "No, a flat house." Whoops, "Oh yeah, right, a flat house—of course."

A single glance from the father suggested a growing interest on his part. The kids gathered around the table; the plane was ready. The beautiful little girl picked it up and sent it on its way to a crash on the floor just as a big woman was rolling her laundry cart toward it. The loud silence ended when the cart and her clunky shoes missed squishing it into the entrance carpet. The three-year-old darted to it. Grabbing it, he sent it on a long perfect glide that had all of us stunned. Even the father's expression turned to a look of amazement. The six-year-old retrieved the plane and with a mighty heave sent it high above the machines past the TV where it fell far out of reach behind the flowerpots.

"Uh-oh!" All three heads spun around toward me with the "What's he going to say now?" look.

"Well, that's the neat thing about paper airplanes, plenty more from where that one came from." Now, even the father seemed interested. A few moments later, with a new paper supply, all three kids were rushing to fold their own planes. Then it happened, the six-year-old looked up at me from his plane making.

Dreams, you know? You know. I had a dream where my grandfather bought a kit of three paper airplanes and some had spikes on them.

I managed a perfunctory "Yeah, I know," but it wasn't needed and there was no time for discussion. All three children were flying their paper airplanes at once. The little girl gazed up at me with an adoring expression that changed her into a beautiful Cinderella and made me feel like her handsome prince. The stern-faced Laundromat attendant brought me back to the real world as she marched past, reluctantly giving us permission to continue by studiously avoiding any eye contact.

The children were having a wonderful time. As I turned to go back to my laundry, the father was at my side. His hand extended into the warmest handshake I could imagine. Time stopped with the quiet strength of his words. "Thank you so much for your kindness." The thank you seemed to go on forever, sustained by his calm steady look of total acceptance that left me in a glow of love that filled my entire being.

The whole experience challenges any casual explanation. At first thought, the experience was a strong example of synchronicity. The little boy needed to talk about a dream he had that morning. How convenient to have a man show up, ready to listen to his dream. On the other hand, I look like a grandfather. Did the boy have a dream of the future where his grandfather symbolized a stranger who would come into his life with paper airplanes? The possibilities increase when we consider that the grandfather in the dream had three paper airplanes and there were three children in the family. Or did the boy actually see me in his dream? He seemed very sure that I knew about dreams. But what about the spikes on the paper airplanes? Next time I go to the Laundromat, I'm going to ask him.

A ROUTINE REQUEST

Billy was small for a five-year-old, but he looked even smaller as he walked into the school's large, unused, high-ceilinged room that had been reserved for testing. He held his mother's hand tightly as he walked quietly with splay-footed awkwardness to the testing table. Billy was next on the list for routine IQ testing. School procedures required IQ scores as a part of the application for special help, although his parents and teacher already knew that his ability level was high enough to qualify. Billy's mom took care of the introductions and then eased herself out of the room.

"How come the other kids don't have to do this?" As little and fragile as he was, Billy showed no hesitation when it came to asking questions as soon as his mother had left. His voice was unusually gruff and sometimes difficult to understand. "Are you wasting my time, because playtime starts now!"

Billy didn't want to take the test, even though most children considered it interesting enough that they didn't complain. As bright as he was, testing presented difficult challenges. He could hardly hold one of the fat pencils designed for younger children. His glasses didn't keep his eyes from wandering when he tried to match designs. He heard directions, but the directions didn't stick in his mind. There were, however, plenty of things that did stick in his mind. During the testing, his throaty voice churned out more questions. "I heard on the news that a planet with people on it crashed and everybody died. Do you think the people who died are still in outer space? Do you know what's in heaven?"

It was time for a break. Billy relished the idea of getting a drink from the hallway water fountain. He was instantly rejuvenated and returned to the testing with renewed energy that lasted all of two minutes. He almost pleaded. "Please say this is the last question. That's all I can do. I'm done." He paused briefly for a breath before his voice turned angry. "Did you ever get pulled over by a policeman? I know what I'd do. You know, I'm strong at breaking stuff and I could break that handle off your briefcase."

Choosing not to respond to his last statement I kept with the assessment requirements and asked Billy if he would please draw a person for me. "Sure, can I draw the insides?"

Caught by surprise, I began wondering about his question as he drew a person with particular attention paid to the digestive tract. A hamburger entered the mouth, wound its way through the stomach and intestine and eventually went out through the person's bottom.

On a hunch, I asked if he had ever been to the hospital.

"Yes." He proceeded to tell a long story of hurting his leg on a nail. I was beginning to believe him before he said that he was just kidding.

His story sounded like a bad dream. "Billy, do you ever remember your dreams?" His answer almost addressed the question.

"My elbow bumped when I woke up and it hurt and I know it's on my body and I know what's inside people's bodies." His husky-sounding voice got louder as he elaborated on his comments about body parts, emphasizing the blood vessels.

Apparently, I needed to be a little more direct. "Billy, do you ever have nightmares?"

Taking my cue, he answered directly, "Yes, when the monster fought me!" He paused long enough for me to ask what happened. He forced an unconvincing smile and said that he had won, but continued describing in detail how the monster brutally stabbed him through the chest with a long knife.

During our discussion, it became more and more obvious that Billy was far from being a typical five-year-old. He was undersized, frightened, and had an endless stream of angry questions. He had poor muscular coordination, visual tracking problems, an unusual voice, speech difficulties, a preoccupation with inner body parts, fears of bodily harm, and terrifying nightmares. Although my job was done, I couldn't ignore this little boy's ongoing pain.

"Billy, how would you really want your nightmare to end; would you like to draw it?" Having children redraw their dreams with happy endings, if done properly, helps them get rid of their nightmares. Billy began drawing a violent and cruel battle with the monster that went on and on and showed no sign of ending. Meanwhile, it really was time for us to stop. My question emerged from desperation. "Billy, we have to stop now; what are you going to do about the monster?"

Billy thought for a moment, his face taken over by a wide-mouthed powerful smile. There was fierceness to his reply. "I'm going to take this picture and tape it next to my bed, so if the monster comes back, he'll be really scared when he looks at the picture and leave quick."

Children are often afraid to confront dream monsters, preferring to avoid them rather than to experience the pain all over again while they're awake. Billy's courage was obvious as he chose to do battle with the monster immediately. Nevertheless, Billy's battle never ended. He will now have a monster that may protect him from other monsters, but we can't be sure that the monster won't again turn on Billy.

If Billy continues to work on the dream at home, like many other children, he may at some point want to kill the monster. If so, he will need to be told that he is not permitted to hurt or kill the monster because dead monsters come back to life in future nightmares, usually bigger and scarier than ever. It would also help to explain to Billy that if he kills the monster, then he is becoming a monster himself. If he still can't figure out a way to deal with the monster, whoever ends up working with Billy may need to tell him that because the dream is his, he can put anyone or anything into his drawing that would be of help.

Billy is quite resourceful and may not have to be told that he can put parents, relatives, friends, superheroes, even friendly monsters into the dream to help him. Of course, the person working with Billy will also have challenges. With such a deserving little person, it would be very tempting to try and help him by making specific suggestions such as making friends with the monster; that would be a rather ideal ending. Unfortunately, that kind of help is misguided and would give Billy the message that he isn't strong enough to come up with a solution on his own.

Just as important is the fact that if Billy isn't given the independence to deal with the monster on his own, the monster will probably show up in future dreams. More than just helping Billy rid himself of nightmares, the described technique of having Billy redraw a dream with an ending that he would want, has the potential to strengthen this little person's identity in a way that will help him feel like a superhero, an important step for a five-year-old.

ALIENS IN THE PARK

I was minding my own business, eating my lunch in a gazebo at the old neighborhood park, quietly reminiscing about years ago when my daughter and I played there together. I imagined myself invisible to avoid any interruptions from a group of boys playing nearby. My strategy didn't work. Before I knew it, one of the boys had come up behind me. He put his arm around my shoulder and gave me a spontaneous, wide, honest-looking but mischievous smile, as if he were my best friend.

Immediately a picture of the kid's grandmother or somebody keeping an eye on the kids from a nearby house window came to mind. I just knew she would think he was up to no good. An older boy had taken in the entire situation, rode his bike right into the gazebo, and in true leader-of-the-pack fashion said, "Can't ya see? He wants to be left alone." So off they went.

In five minutes they were back. Thinking that this might be a dream-gathering opportunity, I told them I was a writer and wrote about dreams, wondering if they'd share some with me. Usually kids are quick to talk about their dreams. So, I was surprised when the youngest boy asked if I was famous. I told them probably not in China. They were hoping to share the limelight with a world famous celebrity.

Trying to get them to talk about dreams, I said a lot of people dream about Spiderman. The oldest boy, about fourteen, agreed, but said he wanted to talk about ghost sightings in the park. The middle boy said that he dreamt about Batman, but with a worried look on his face, admitted that Batman was always the bad guy in his dreams. A younger boy just stood there keeping quiet.

The fourteen-year-old was becoming more impatient and looking quite intense. He said, "I'm even more afraid of aliens!" and described ghost-like creatures with weird oval-shaped heads and scary slots for eyes. The other boys joined in by talking about red lights from spacecraft that had been seen in the park. They added that the lights had been written up in the local newspaper.

With disgust, one of the boys complained, "They said it was just a balloon, but I don't believe it." Just as suddenly as the boys had started talking, they stopped. It was like a mist of fear had settled over them. Clearly, the boys were just going to talk about their daydreams.

I encouraged the boys to talk more about their fear of aliens asking how they could find out if there really were aliens in the park. Before long, they were really into it, planning an adventure of camping out at night in the park to meet aliens. They would get to see for themselves if the aliens were real.

The topic finally exhausted itself. My time with the boys was coming to a close, leaving all of us feeling a bit let down. With no more to talk about, we quietly said our good-byes. As I began slowly walking away, I heard one of the boys call out hopefully, "You going to write a story about us?" I turned and looking back, said that I would. The next question came in a doubtful tone, "Do you want our names?" It didn't take long for them to tell me: Andre, Juan, and Jordan. By this time I was halfway across the park, and just barely heard the last question. It was wishful. "Do you come here much?"

One of the reasons I like talking with children about dreams is that I get the chance to help them deal with their fears that are often in the form of monsters or other kinds of scary things. In doing so, children gain a positive and powerful inner strength. The children don't know that in talking about those monsters and figuring out how to deal with them, they are actually practicing how to deal with waking-life monsters, such as the bullies and the "big shots" they'll encounter all through life. They are developing powerful tools for living: self-respect, self-confidence, and self-compassion. But in the park, it wasn't about facing monsters in nighttime dreams. It was about facing monsters in daydreams that had taken on the stature of "real life" monsters. With my help, the boys did an admirable job of facing the aliens. As a result, the boys will be better able to face their dream monsters. Having decided to confront "real life" aliens, dealing with a bad guy Batman from a dream should be piece of cake.

This story illustrates that the role of the dream gatherer is much more than just that of an observer or a simple recorder of other people's dreams. All three boys realized that I was a safe person with whom they could explore their fears. Our quickly developed comradery was one of a transitory yet lasting nature that can be expected to have a positive, ongoing ripple effect on our lives as well as the lives of others. Much time could be spent analyzing that experience in the park. I prefer to treat the experience like a dream, by allowing the future meanings and value of the situation to unfold over time.

The universe is sure to provide the boys and me with growth-producing experiences that will build on that park experience. In the future, if one of those experiences involves meeting aliens, we'll be ready.

Arthur Strock, Ph.D.

DINOSAURS AREN'T REAL

Bruce had just turned thirteen. He was a likeable, well-mannered, tall, gangly boy with oversized limbs and a body that kept moving and never stopped. His penetrating eyes searched for my reaction to his battling with himself to stop the incessant fidgeting and wriggling around in his chair, a battle that he eventually lost. His chair crashed to the floor and left him crouching over it with a confused look on his face that changed into the inquisitive and searching look of a puppy who knows he's guilty of something, but isn't quite sure what. It was time for me to deflect guilt. "Yeah, chairs do that sometimes."

Bruce was one of the most active boys I had ever seen. I wondered what kind of dreams he had. He welcomed the chance to tell me.

Night after night, a long time ago, I dreamt of dinosaurs. I was in bed in the dream, but the T Rex looked at me through the window and started roaring at me, and it was scary. I cried every night and my parents would come into my room. I told them, "A dinosaur tried to eat me."

My parents had the answer. "Dinosaurs aren't real; everything's going to be fine."

I eventually got over those dinosaurs, but then the monsters came and they tried to eat me too. And there was a crazy dream where I was a cookie and a monster ate my leg.

When I was little, the only way I could get away from the monsters was to jump off something very high. Somehow I would get myself to the top of tall things like buildings. It wasn't funny coming down. I'd go splat on the concrete, but it would wake me up and I'd finally be away from the monsters. Now I just fly.

Bruce elaborated on his dream life. His dreams of terrifying dinosaurs and monsters that would wake him up and leave him crying for help were still very much alive and vivid in his mind. Unfortunately, his parents, like most parents, wanted to help, but didn't understand that the reality of dream life can be far more real than the reality of waking life, especially for children. The reassurance given by Bruce's parents was a version of the ever-popular comment that has been used by parents for generations, "Don't worry, it was just a dream." Bruce took their reassurance to heart that dinosaurs weren't real. His parents' reassurance resulted in the disappearance of the dinosaurs, but monsters then took the place of the dinosaurs.

Bruce explained how his dreams also changed in another way. He continued to wake up, but not fully. He woke up within the dream and was able to combine a waking awareness with his dream awareness, a process called lucid dreaming. In such dreams, he developed an escape strategy of jumping off high things. Over time, in order to avoid crashing to the ground, he taught himself to fly.

When asked what he would wish for now regarding his dreams Bruce said, "Now I fly, but I would want to upgrade my dreams. I would set them up so people don't get on my case."

"Why don't you decide to do just that?"

Bruce's "No" answer was given without thought as his body resumed its incessant fidgeting while he fumbled in his pocket for his smart phone. He wanted to show me pictures of all the cars he wanted to own.

Bruce's remarks about people getting on his case suggest that the dream monsters have been replaced by people in his dreams who tell him to calm down and stop being so hyper. When he does decide to commit himself to a dream upgrade, he will be able to use his lucid dreaming skills to develop strategies for dealing with his hyperactive behavior in everyday life, allowing him to become more relaxed, happier, and more productive.

His dream solutions may well be symbolic or a play on words. Just like he learned to fly to get away from the monsters, he may be able to take a magic pill to slow down so people won't always be on his case.

WAITING IN LINE

We're always waiting in line for something. If the line's long enough, the old and historically irritating recommendation to "wait patiently" may come to mind. And who wants to wait patiently? On this occasion I was waiting in line at Staples.

"I know you! I know you." A beautiful, bouncy, exquisitely groomed girl in line behind me was jumping up and down with excitement. "You're the dream guy!" Turning to her friend, she said, "He's the one I told you about who talked about dreams at my school and can tell you exactly what your dreams mean." The difference in appearance between the two girls was striking. The girl who remembered me was short and stocky with shiny jet-black hair, while her friend was tall and slender with vivid, bright red hair.

The girl's friend joined in, "Oh I dream all the time." I asked if she'd had any weird ones lately. Try as she could, no dreams came to her mind. The pause was quickly filled by the first girl's rapid-fire telling of a dream that involved her going into the laundry room of another friend's house. The washing machine was doing something with juice but because she spoke so rapidly, the dream didn't seem to make any kind of sense. She stopped talking as quickly as she had started and waited expectantly for an instant interpretation.

We know that dream interpretation doesn't work that way. I was trying to figure out what to say about the dream as I juggled a rewards card, a discount coupon, a credit card; sign the signature pad; and listen to comments from the cashier. I was also aware that it was past closing time and the employees wanted to go home. What a nightmare. Forgetting that she was a child for a moment, I blurted out a question about whether or not something needed to be changed in her life.

Her response was immediate. The vibrant excitement was gone, replaced with a blank stare and a very quiet "No." She was suddenly so still that I realized I must have touched a nerve. She had turned inward and must have been focused on a life problem and how the dream was related to it. Her dream may have been related to snacks and soft drinks, her parents, maybe even her girlfriend. She suddenly seemed to return to the present, and without saying anything rejoined her dad and friend.

Thanks to the patient cashier we got through the line and were all walking quickly out of the store when the second girl remembered a dream. She had dreamt about a family on a television show and wanted to know what it meant. I asked what the family was like. The girl sadly announced that they all looked really good. She started to explain how she looked in comparison, but her voice just trailed off.

Knowing I had just a few seconds, I appealed to the need that every child has to look and feel special. I suggested that just before going to bed that night she look in the mirror and know that without any TV or Hollywood makeup artist, she was just right the way she was. She responded with a charming smile that brought her to life as she skipped off with her friend.

There had been no time to be impatient with the checkout process. There had been no boredom encouraging us to buy unneeded stuff displayed at the cash register. There had been no temptation to reach for an iPhone. Dream sharing allowed us to be alive in the present. The children even got the extra attention that they crave so much in these electronic times. And while doing dreamwork on the run isn't ideal, I felt that I had at least offered something to each of them that was useful. And if all goes according to plan, both girls will feel a bit better about themselves and be able to put aside some of their worries.

RELATIONSHIPS

The Better Life

THE BETTER LIFE

Even twenty-five years ago, the old bakery located on a small street next to an abandoned railroad siding was too nondescript to look like a bakery. The large front windows didn't display anything and were too dark to see through. The old display cases inside had some scattered cookies and calzones in them, but Santini's Bakery had been known for its delicious Italian bread. Behind the counters, the shelves were always stocked with freshly made bread in all different shapes and sizes. On Fridays there were stacks of readymade pizza dough. It was always an adventure to go in for olive oil and pizza makings and chat with old Mr. Santini. His two sisters would be there, sitting quietly at the side of the room watching with their beautiful, alluring, dark eyes that held intrigue from many decades of living.

Years later I ended up going out of my way to pass the old bakery. Worn out bread-making equipment had been thrown to the side of the building, now as useless as an abandoned rusted-out old car. An electrician's truck was parked in front near a new Mercedes sedan. Rumor had it that a man who had done very well for himself and didn't want for money had just purchased the place. The temptation to go inside and take a look was too great to resist.

There were all new cases and new shelves behind them. A peek through a doorway into the unlit back room where the bread had been made revealed outlines of new equipment, wires, and cables. At the same time, a hint of light and some indistinguishable music drew my attention to a half-open door by the side of the front room. Mr.Santini was gone, but inside, a large, husky man with salt-and-pepper hair and a matching old-world mustache sat unmoving at a littered desk displaying pictures of children of all different ages.

He looked distant, but just friendly enough to risk a quietly spoken, "Hey what's the story, are you the new owner? He nodded and with a gesture invited me in, pointing to the chair next to his desk. His vague expression prompted me to begin. "You still sell great olive oil here?"

Color seemed to come to his face as he began slowly. "My brother and them are picking the olives right now. They'll be getting the honey too from the wild bees." Alexio reached into a desk drawer and shuffled through a pack of pictures and pulled one out, an amazing beehive with multi-tiered wax combs attached to a large tree trunk. "We'll be getting honey too. How are you doing? Wife and kids?"

I gave the obligatory everything's going well while adding a new twist, "And the book I'm writing about dreams is coming along too."

A look of anguish replaced the beginning of a welcoming smile. His voice sounded older than his years. "I dream of all the old people. Sometimes I think I'm going crazy. I still see my village. I remember every path where they went, which fields were good for the vegetables, where the hives were to get the honey, and the small houses where everyone lived." Alexio didn't look at me. He was revisiting his old village in Crete as it had been over fifty years before.

Sounding resigned, he went on. "When I was a kid—well it's all different now. We'd sleep outside, yeah, under a tree. My brother and I had to walk five miles just to get to school. We would walk through a stream and wash ourselves off. After school we would walk back to the house and go right to the barrel, reach in and grab a handful of olives and stuff them in our pockets. Then we'd go in the house and get a hunk of cheese and some bread and start walking to the fields to work, with the water from the olives dripping down our legs. We didn't have shoes." Alexio looked up at me. "I was eleven years old before I got my first pair of shoes and I had to work weeks to pay for them. And the whole town would celebrate the saints' days with gatherings and dancing. Weddings took days to celebrate. We were all there, eight brothers and sisters.

"I left home when I was twelve after I graduated from grammar school. I told my dad I wanted a better life. I was crying. He was crying too. He asked me where I was going. He gave me money, a large amount for him, I remember—three dollars. I had to walk as far as from here to Brooklyn to get to the coast where I could board a boat to Athens. When I went to get a ticket, I showed the man the money I had. He wouldn't take it, wrote his name on a piece of paper and said, 'When you get on the boat, go to the kitchen.'" The old businessman was smiling at the recollection.

"I got a big bowl of spaghetti. After getting off the boat I went to where they were building. A man saw me and said, 'What do you want here, kid?'

"'I want to work.'

"'What can you do?'

"'Anything you can do.' The men on the job stopped, gathered around us looking at me. 'I can push a wheelbarrow, twist metal, and mix concrete; done it all in my village.' The foreman looked at the other men, nodded his head and gave the okay.

"I worked. I slept on the unfinished concrete floors at night. In the morning, I was up early and had the plywood forms up by the time the men arrived. Because I was there so early, the foreman asked me where I lived. I told him: in town. One night I heard a motorcycle come onto the worksite. The motor stopped and then in the silence there was the sound of shuffling feet and a flashlight beam aimed right at me. It was the foreman, 'Why did you lie to me?'

I told him, 'I didn't want anybody to feel sorry for me. I had to make it on my own.'

"His answer was direct, 'You're coming home with me.' I got on the back of his motorcycle. When we got to his house, he spoke with his wife. Looking at me, she started to cry.

"Later, I worked on ships and jumped ship at Hoboken. I was sixteen then. Found work at a restaurant washing dishes—twelve hour days, thirty dollars a week."

Alexio looked up and said quietly, "Seven dollars a week for my room. At night, I'd walk into that room, pull the light chain and see cockroaches covering the walls."

Nothing else he had said carried with it such pain of hardship.

"I'd left a bag of potato chips open. There must have been five million cockroaches in that bag." His head and body involuntarily shuddered. His whole body remembered the horror of the sight. "Look," he said pointing to his arm, "The hairs are standing up."

I made a comment about a lot of Greeks working in restaurants in those days. He gave a knowing smile and said the immigration officials were around almost every week looking for illegal immigrants they could send back.

He could have gone on, but stopped, rummaged through a desk drawer, pulled out a soiled mini spiral pad and asked me to jot down my name and telephone number. He said nothing, but I knew he wanted to make sure I ended up with some special olive oil and honey from his old village.

The man had accomplished his goal set when he was only twelve years old. He had struggled and entered the better life that now he apparently found empty. He didn't discuss dreams of fear, physical pain, or even monstrous cockroaches, the type of dreams that accompany posttraumatic stress. He chose to talk about dreams that reflected the childhood memories filled with hardship but meaningful connections with people, a call for him to search for the love and connectedness in his present life that he had felt as a child and as a young man.

He was starting on yet another business venture, still following the mirage of the better life. A part of him longed for the old world, more physically demanding but more comforting than his new Mercedes. He looked tired, as if he wanted to call it quits. If he could fade back into the past, he might look for an old pair of leather shoes, get on a boat for Crete, and then walk back to the village of his youth where he had been truly alive. Hopefully, he will at least find joy in being with the children whose pictures are on his desk and find relief from the dreams that remind him of his lost childhood.

I'd never heard Mr. Santini and his sisters speak of their youth. But like Alexio, we can be sure that their old world memories had become embedded in dreams that had many reruns during their long waking hours.

MY HUSBAND WON'T DO IT!

Emily, a friend of a friend, shows up in my life every few years. This time it was at a luncheon. "Arthur, I saved you a seat. I was hoping you'd be here. I had this dream I wanted to ask you about."

Emily is always very proper, but that day she looked really tired. Her appearance was a reminder of the light brown and cream sepia photographs taken in the 1930s. Her tinted light tan hair matched her outdated thin jacket-like top and skirt, an outfit that also looked tired from years of being worn on semi-special occasions.

"We have a garage. It's filthy—totally jammed—filled with bags of garbage, rusty old garden rakes and shovels, broken equipment, old ripped bags of smelly fertilizer, boxes of my husband's old tools, and has dirt all over the floor. I just hired a cleaning lady for the house. Never had one before. She thought our kitty litter was mouse dirt. I had to take her into the garage to prove to her that it wasn't by showing her the kitty litter that had spilled from the bags. It was so embarrassing.

"Last week I had this dream:

I'm cleaning up the garage with all the old lawnmowers and wheelbarrows and bags of stuff to recycle. I'm so angry that I stop.

But Emily recalled that she didn't stop being angry after she woke up. "Last year, it was the basement. I finally hired someone to take out all the dirty cartons, old rotting plywood paneling, and the old floor tile. I have seven grown daughters and a son. All of their old stuff had to be cleared out too.

"My husband wouldn't do anything, but once I hired a man to do the job, my husband took over, made like it was all his idea, chatted with the man, and directed him every step of the way. Luckily for me, the man was very patient.

"I've asked my husband to do something about the garage again and again. He says he will but never does. He's eighty-three now and doesn't fix things or do anything the way he used to. He built our first house, did all the carpentry and electrical wiring, but just doesn't get to the garage. He's forgetful too."

Emily then began recounting all of the possibilities open to her for getting the garage cleaned up, explaining in detail why each plan wouldn't work. She seemed exhausted and looked like she needed relief just from thinking about the futility of it all.

Emily's deceptively simple dream provides several clues to help recognize when a dream is far more important than it may seem. Most dreams are remembered for only a brief time. Emily's dream was remembered with clarity for days. Emotions in dreams are usually replaced by emotional reactions to the immediacy of waking life.

Emily's anger in the dream stayed alive in waking life, even reminding her of other similar situations from the past. How the dream is told is also significant. Usually dreamers blurt out the dream first and have to be reminded that dreams are related to life events. Emily, however, took great care and time in explaining her life situation even before telling the dream. Symbols can provide the key to understanding a dream. Not so in this case. The garage was the garage. And finally, understanding the meaning of a dream often provides a comforting sense of closure, but there had been no sense of closure for Emily.

I began to share with Emily what I thought was happening in the dream. "Emily, could your husband's forgetting about the garage be protecting him from trying to do something that deep down inside he knows he just can't do any more?"

Our conversation was abruptly interrupted by someone who had known Emily years ago and wanted to say hello. Then came the hustle and bustle of the waitress making sure everyone got what they had ordered, followed by the business of eating. Finally the dessert arrived.

Apparently our conversation was not over. Emily turned, looked at me and in the softest tone of voice said, "I'm going to call someone to clear out the garage and ask my Harold if he'll supervise."

A VOICE FROM THE PAST

Betty, an attractive, spontaneous, smartly dressed, secretary and devoted mother of two pre-adolescent girls, was in the middle of a divorce. As I entered the office, she gave an open-faced, wide-eyed smile. "I had a call from an ex-boyfriend of twenty-seven years ago. He was really the love of my life. It triggered a dream."

There was a kitten in a bucket of water and the feeling was not to kill it but to hide it.

She kept talking, not even breathing between sentences. "I analyzed it myself. I looked up all the symbols. Water is emotions, it meant comfort because it was clear and it spilled over. A kitten means betrayal and trouble. A pail means a better life, riches overflowing, increased life quality. A handkerchief in a triangle partly over the face is significant because it means a separation from a significant other. Big eyes stand for looking at a significant issue. The handle meant that it's holding the bucket of prosperity. I was the power. Wet means close to the surface and the kitten was white meaning innocence and simplicity in the situation. I know you don't believe in dream dictionaries, but mine was right on. The meaning of all those symbols put together meant I should stay away from him."

Betty was excited but ambivalent about getting the call. "He's on his second marriage which is failing. He asked me if I had ever been unhappy and wanted to know if I wanted his telephone number." Betty commented that he sounded much different from how she remembered him and considered his request to be inappropriate.

At the same time, the call also brought up the feelings of young love and the loss she had experienced when they broke up at age eighteen. Although she wanted to experience that love again, she said with forced conviction that she knew it wouldn't be possible. She also said she was thankful that she was now able to ground herself, draw upon her adult maturity and wisdom, and focus on the positive aspects of her current life.

Despite Betty's affirmations, she couldn't get the past out of her mind and continued thinking out loud. "The call triggered the dream. I had thought about him and wondered how things would have turned out if we'd gotten married. But just hearing him let me know that it wouldn't have worked. I'm not going to think about him anymore. Because of the dream, I can put my thoughts to rest. Thank goodness you mentioned the value of dreams when you first started working here."

Betty's rapid discussion of the dream symbols had left little time to ask questions. She remembered what I had said about dream dictionaries, that they have limited value. Checking a dream dictionary entry for the meaning of a dream is like checking a friend's text message reply in response to an important life question. They both fall short of the need for an in-depth investigation.

Dream content and symbolic meanings come in reference to the dreamer's ongoing life history and emotional reactions to a situation. A dream dictionary is more likely to be the result of the author's own life associations or at best a reflection of current research involving the frequency of common dream symbols. I no longer tell people to throw out their dream dictionaries. When we're really stuck and can't see how a dream relates to our situation, a dream dictionary, like an overzealous friend, might provide a helpful clue to get us unstuck. It was beyond me how Betty arrived at her interpretation. Even so, her decision to avoid rekindling a relationship with a past boyfriend when both of them were still married to other people seemed like a good idea and a good way of keeping herself out of trouble.

HE'S GOT TO PEE ALL THE TIME

A shift in office staff resulted in my seeing very little of Betty for almost three years. Quite unexpectedly, she showed up one day and mentioned that her divorce had been finalized and that she had been living with her also-divorced high school sweetheart for the past two years. She described Bob as her soulmate with whom she was very happy, but wanted to investigate the dream with me as opposed to using the dream dictionary she had been enthusiastic about in the past.

I'm in a New York deli and walk past the cold cut counter. I'm with my boyfriend who said to me, "I need to use the bathroom." So, he goes to the bathroom and I walk over to one of the tables to sit down and wait—he's got to pee all the time. All of a sudden, this big guy with a big gun enters the deli. I quick hide under one of the tables. I'm holding my breath looking at his big chunky feet in sandals and then I wake up.

Having given the dream considerable thought, Betty said that the dream was frightening because it so closely reminded her of a man in the news who had recently killed someone in a delicatessen. She added that she was so scared in the dream that she woke up holding her breath. While telling the dream, she hesitated and chuckled as she mentioned the cold cut counter, "Bob's always got to pee all the time—high blood pressure pills."

Could the dream have been related to the foods that she and Bob were eating? Betty didn't think so. Because she seemed to pay special attention to the terrorist's chunky feet and sandals, I asked if they might provide a clue to the dream's meaning. That question didn't produce any leads either.

The critical clue to the dream's meaning lay in how animated Betty had become when she described her boyfriend's need to "pee all the time." During our discussion, she explained that Bob's continual need to pee had gotten a lot of laughs and had achieved the status of an in-house joke.

Looking for the symbolic meaning of objects can often lead to dead ends as it did in this case. Betty's excitement at mentioning Bob's frequent need to urinate drew attention to the in-house joke as a possible key to understanding the dream. Family jokes are rarely pure fun, but sometimes provide a socially acceptable way of sweeping relationship issues under the rug. In the dream, Betty felt all alone and in danger, while her boyfriend was totally out of the picture attending to his own needs. My question for Betty was whether the dream was calling attention to that pattern in their waking life. I wondered if Betty was concerned that Bob might not be available for her when she needed physical or emotional support. As she listened to me, her face lit up in surprise. Her reply could have been heralded by the sound of a gong.

"That's a wow. That's fantastic. That's the problem with our relationship." After a subdued and thoughtful moment Betty said, "You know what? I just had an 'aha' moment. Your way is better than the cookie-cutter interpretations in my dream dictionary."

I LOVE ANIMALS

Sometimes requests for dreams result in no discussion of dreams at all. The result, however, may be just as interesting as hearing a dream; it may be like living a dream.

While driving home from the International Association for the Study of Dreams Annual Conference, dream sharing was uppermost in my mind. At a gas station stop along the way, my partner Susan got out of the car and started toward the convenience store. In the car next to ours, a small dog was sitting in the middle of an enormous woman's lap. Seeing Susan, the little dog started an ear-piercing nonstop yapping.

The driver, who was out of the car pumping gas, turned and called out an apology. "He doesn't know you."

Seeing an opportunity for dream sharing, I playfully called out to the dog as I got out of our car, "But you know me"—hoping the comment would be a conversation opener with the driver. The little dog just barked louder.

The driver, looking like a misplaced hippy from the sixties, came out from between the gas pumps and hushed his dog. He was about 5' 8" and wore a soft brimmed camo-style military hat that hid the beginning of a waist long, carefully knotted ponytail of straight white hair that fit in with his weathered, rugged-looking, leathery face. That face with its purposeful eyes was even more memorable for its sparse and wispy white beard. His sleeveless, olive drab T-shirt was thin and torn from many washings, but did its best to cover a very large belly that disappeared into an equally worn and faded pair of pants.

The man had tattoos on each of his big arms: a skull inside a spider web on one arm and a tired-looking deer with a small red heart in its center on the other arm. As he turned to face me, another little dog in the car suddenly appeared. Up popped his little black-and-white-spotted head to peer at me through the window.

By this time, I had started to pump gas, but took the time to ask the man about his dreams. "You ever have dreams about these little dogs?"

The response was fast, but had nothing to do with my question. "I love animals. There's a third dog in the car. I have eight dogs. I rescue animals. Animals come right up to me. Deer will walk right up to me; that's why I don't hunt."

I wanted to know more about this tough-looking, soft-spoken man. I asked about his tattoos, pointing to the ones I had seen on his arms. He showed little interest in discussing the old tattoos, but pointing to his forearm, he turned it to show me a new and beautifully accurate portrait of the sweet little black-and-white dog who was now watching us intently. The man then changed the subject by showing me a carefully cupped hand. He touched his hand gently as he told his story of rescuing and nursing a tiny newborn rabbit whose mother had died giving birth. With a smile of self-acceptance that almost covered his yellowed decaying teeth, he said with quiet pride and dignity, "I returned it to the wild when it got old enough."

He gave me a quick look as he replaced the gas cap and got into the driver's seat of his car. His expression had turned very business-like. Cutting through the hoarseness that comes with old age, he gave his proclamation, "I'm different than everybody else. See? I drive on the right-hand side." The car's steering wheel was in fact on the right-hand side. The out-of-place steering wheel in the rusting old Toyota made it look like it had come from a dream. The car jerked forward and over the rattles and cough of the muffler came the man's call, "Have a good day." I was watching the last fadeout scene in an old Western movie where the hero, after saving the day, rides off into the sunset.

As I got back into my car, I felt as if I had been dreaming. Not just the man, but everything had seemed different: the huge woman, the ancient car, even the little black-and-white dog with its dreamlike Alice-in-Wonderland quality of popping up from nowhere.

Because the experience was so much like a dream, I decided to treat it like a dream and look for its message. Because dreams parallel our waking lives, I explored the situation in the context of coming from a conference in which I had met friends and made meaningful connections with strangers.

In the situation at the gas pump, I once again made a meaningful connection. It didn't matter that the man and I hadn't discussed dreams. Asking about his dreams had provided the man with what he really needed, someone to talk with who, by listening, would validate his love of animals and his need to be different. Interpreting the experience like a dream provided a clear message. Dream sharing is a vehicle for making meaningful connections with others, and not an end in itself.

DECISION MAKING

A Window of Opportunity

A WINDOW OF OPPORTUNITY

Going through the ground-level entrance door of Hometown Printing activated the familiar bell alerting Glen that a customer had just entered. I knew he was on duty. His old car, complete with the ever-present kayak on top, was in the parking lot. Glen was a fixture with the company, having been there almost twenty-five years since his graduation from high school. His wheelchair zipped into view from the back room as Glen propelled himself to the front counter with his usual look of purposeful determination.

"Simple job, Glen; I just need a couple of copies of my logo from this zip drive." He took the zip drive and was back quickly with my copies. Looking at the colorful "Live by Your Dreams" logo reminded him of the dream that woke him up at 5:00 that morning, a dream that he was quick to share with me.

I was going back to my old high school that had been completely refurbished. The administrators were all new, so I didn't recognize anyone, but I was determined to register for classes.

Glen didn't elaborate on the dream, but began talking about the early morning radio talk show that he had listened to when he couldn't get back to sleep. His wheelchair edged back a bit when I returned to the subject of his dream, asking why in the dream he was going back to high school rather than grade school or college. For just a moment he looked trapped, but recovered quickly, saying that he frequently has high school dreams, but the high school officials always turned him away saying, "You're too old for high school."

Glen's facial expression was empty. "I've been thinking about going back to college for years." He brightened, "No charge for the two copies."

As I walked out the door, I could see why he had been thinking about college for years. Dead ahead was the unavoidable sight of the gleaming gold cupola of the local college's administration building.

During my next visit, I asked Glen if he was still thinking about college. He commented that there are government programs that are designed to help college hopefuls who have disabilities. "Maybe someday."

Although Glen is intelligent and quick thinking, it was hardly surprising that he avoided any discussion of college. Being an older college student presents its own problems, but for Glen, even the most routine task of living could develop into a time-consuming challenge. He lived his life from a wheelchair except when he somehow pulled his kayak from the car and lifted his body and unmoving legs into the boat to go fishing.

Dream messages, however, are known to come with perfect timing. Glen's recurring dream suggests that the universe has a plan for him and that he has a window of opportunity for applying to colleges and most likely getting accepted. Symbolically his dream's message, that he is too old for high school, may reflect a common fear of being unable to make the grade as an older student in an academic setting. He must wonder also if he is up to the challenge physically. At a deeper level, it would be surprising if Glen has not wanted for a long time to go to college. His school dreams may end, but as long as they hint at attending college, his window of opportunity is still open.

WHAT TO SERVE AT THE DINNER PARTY

A friend of mine wanted to talk with me about a dream in which the President of the United States spoke with her. But by the time we got together, her dream of the President took second place. "I had a crazy dream last night."

> *I was hosting a party, not at my place, but a big house. I was glad to see the people, but I was worried I didn't have enough food. I was worried that they wouldn't like the fish I was preparing too.*

When asked what the dream of hosting a party might mean, she replied, "I worry sometimes that I'm becoming too much of a hermit and should reach out to others."

Trying to lighten the air, I playfully I asked, "What's this worry about serving fish all about?" Emma said that she loves fish, but doesn't serve it to others because so many people don't like it. Emma's somber tone of voice let me know that her dream was far more serious than it had seemed.

Emma, almost always wrapped in an invisible cloak of silence, seemed at a loss to explain more about the dream. When asked to identify a theme of the dream, she wondered if she had been a "giving-enough person." Her statement was at odds with her compassionate nature. Neither did it fit with her past careers in nursing and social work. At a deeper level, however, Emma may have been concerned about being rejected and not worthy enough to have a dinner party at not just any house, but at a big house.

An important aspect of Emma's dream was that it offered her an alternative to being socially reclusive. In the dream, she had done something she did not normally do: she had reached out socially by inviting people to dinner. I asked if she might want to honor the dream by hosting a dinner party. Her smile was like a time-release picture of a flower coming into bloom. "That would be a good thing for me to do."

Setting out to change one's lifestyle is more difficult than it might seem. So I looked forward to learning if Emma had taken a step forward that would allow her to become more social. Seeing her a few months later, she enthusiastically recalled her dinner party and how much of a success it had been. Because she had been worried in her dream that she wouldn't have enough food for everyone, I asked about it. She was tickled by my question and reassured me that there had been more than enough. And when I playfully asked again about the fish and whether or not she had served it, Emma laughed out loud eyes twinkling, "You know I didn't—but I did serve it to myself the night after the party, and got nothing but compliments."

Emma's decision to honor the dream by inviting people to dinner had paid rich dividends. She enjoyed a social success and was visibly feeling more satisfied with herself. Both literally and figuratively, by feeding people she was also able to satisfy her continuing need to be a giving person.

GRADUATE CLASSES

Ed is a good friend of mine, an accountant who has his own tax service. Years ago we got into a pattern of having lunch together every month or so to make sure we kept our friendship alive. We alternate between a couple of spots that are convenient for both of us. Ed recalls his dreams nearly every night, has more than a casual interest in them, and likes to share them with me during our luncheon get-togethers. Recently, however, Ed gave me a call about getting together before our usual time. At the restaurant, he wasn't as relaxed as usual and said that he needed my ideas on what he called a "repetitive" dream that he found extremely upsetting. Right after ordering, with his emotions under cover, he related the dream in his usual very objective and often understated manner.

I am pursuing a graduate degree at State College where I got my undergraduate degree. I am very fearful of missing classes and am unsure as to how many credits I have earned. I repeatedly go to the registrar's office to get a copy of my classes so I know on what days each course is held.

Ed's dream was a good example of what is considered to be one of the most common universal dream themes: poor performance vs good performance. I knew we needed to determine which performance-related aspect of his life was triggering the dream.

There was nothing particularly bothersome going on in his life that was family-or health-related. But because my dad had been an accountant, I knew that Ed would be dreading the rapidly approaching income tax deadline date of April fifteenth.

"Well Ed, I'm wondering if the dream could be job related. After all, it's getting into tax season, and I bet you'll have a lot of tax returns to prepare." Ed was silent. He needed more detail to consider how my comment was related to his dream. "We know it pays to look for plays on words. The word credits may provide a clue. Debits and credits are pretty important to you accountants. I know you're not taking any classes at the moment, but tax credits sure aren't things to miss. How do you keep up to date on all that stuff?"

Ed had the look on his face he'd get when he was hunting for something in one of his big tax manuals. He began slowly. "Arthur, you may have hit on something. I have a new tax software program that I have some anxiety about and, in essence, I am taking classes learning it on my own, on a daily basis. There are several new tax credits available this year that I cannot afford to miss. Very interesting. Good analysis, Doc." Ed had been working very hard mentally. It was good to see his mild-mannered smile return.

Conscientious people like my friend Ed are very likely to have performance dreams. Many such dreams occur in a classroom setting. The level of the classes, and where and when they're held are important symbolically. Ed's classes are at a graduate level, indicating a higher-level learning than might be had in the grades or at the college level. The fact that the classes are being held at State College provides waking realism to the dream. Ed's associating his learning with taking classes on an everyday basis also shows how important the issue is in his waking life.

My responses also illustrate how we interpret the dreamer as well as the dream. In this case, my knowledge of the stress that accountants go through during tax season helped me to ask Ed relevant questions. I suspect he got relief from his worries by admitting his job-related fears openly to himself and to me. Having dealt with the issue, he can expect his repetitive dream to end. He'll have more energy available for learning the new tax software and be less likely to miss those new tax credits. Now that's a win-win bottom line and a good advertisement for productive dreamwork in the business sector.

Arthur Strock, Ph.D.

THE RIGHT JOB

Gail's cute bob of a haircut and always upbeat, cheerful style almost concealed her qualities of perseverance, focus, and diligence. We'd known each other for a couple of years as members of a community services organization and had exchanged dreams. Gail was an assistant professor at a local college in the funeral services department. I knew that she was devoted to her job and was loved and respected by her colleagues and students.

At one of our meetings, I playfully asked, "How're ya dreamin?" Her somber response was unexpected, "The problem is, I'm not dreaming." Gail was clearly upset. Because of her teaching excellence, she had just been asked to assume the role of department chairman. She explained that her joy in life was teaching. Department chairmen did little teaching. But the real problem was a college mandate requiring the dismissal of any faculty member who turned down such a promotion. She would be without a job if she turned down the promotion. Looking downcast, Gail's voice was barely audible as she alluded to how she usually relied on her dreams to help her with difficult problems, but her dreams had shut down.

Gail called me a few days later saying that she had kept asking for dream guidance before going to sleep and was happy to report that her dream machine was working again.

I dreamt that I was a tailor. I was trying to change a woman's wedding dress that someone else had made and was a poor fit. Try as I might, I couldn't get the dress to fit. The woman thought I, the tailor, knew her well, but I didn't. I wondered why she had come to me to fit a dress that I hadn't even made in the first place.

During the call, Gail puzzled over how a tailor and a wedding dress could have anything to do with her waking-life desire to keep teaching future morticians. I suggested that as a way of getting closer to an interpretation, she have an imaginary conversation with the dream woman in the wedding dress and get to know her better.

At the next community meeting, Gail had her sparkle back. She had followed my advice. Although her imaginary conversation with the dream woman had left her without helpful information, it had triggered another dream:

The woman in the wedding dress reappeared. We sat together on a park bench. I asked her, "Who are you?"

The woman said, "I am your passion for teaching," I put my arm around the woman and felt a tear roll down my cheek.

"Arthur, because of that dream, I stuck to my guns. I turned down the promotion. And guess what? They're going to keep me anyway and I get to continue teaching."

Dreams provide information in support of our emotional needs. Gail didn't understand her first dream. As often happens when a dream doesn't make sense to the dreamer or is misunderstood, an additional dream presents itself to give clarification. Gail's second dream provided additional information that gave her the courage to make a career decision based on her desire to be true to herself and follow her joy.

Exploring the symbolic meanings in both dreams helps to confirm that Gail's decision to stick with her career goals was in her best interests. The woman from the first dream in the wedding dress and subsequently sitting with Gail on a park bench in the second dream was an archetypal figure representing Gail's higher or wise self.

The written account of the dream also has other symbols that contain embedded meanings that are significant beyond the visual images that they portray. The wedding dress symbolized the job of department chairman, a job that would not be a good fit for Gail. Sitting on a park bench is an idiomatic expression often used to describe a person out of work, a situation that was feared, but did not materialize. The tears shared with her wise self symbolized the relief she would feel when she affirmed the importance and value of more fully recognizing and satisfying her own needs. Most important, Gail shows how an accomplished dreamworker can use dreams as an aid in making pivotal life decisions.

Arthur Strock, Ph.D.

APPLES AND ORANGES

It had been three years since our lake community's disastrous mudslide wiped out two homes on the hill above the lake. Not nearly enough as compensation, but appreciated nevertheless, was the mud's demolition of an old abandoned waterfront restaurant complete with its pervasive smell of mildew and mold.

The township had made plans to build an elaborate pavilion on the site of the old restaurant and the work had finally begun on one of the hottest days of the year. A man was using an iron bar to dislodge stones from holes for the pavilion footings. It was locally thought that the ground was so tough to dig, anyone doing so deserved an award.

"I bet you're glad you have that iron bar for working the ground here," I said.

"I'd rather have a different kind of bar." After a mutual chuckle, he opened up, saying he'd been a marine serving in Iraq and Afghanistan and had learned, "Ya just have to flex. Ya gotta do things you don't want to do."

Wanting to ask him about his dreams, I continued, "I bet you've seen and done things that you couldn't have imagined before, but over there it seems that violence is an everyday event."

Instead of answering, he asked if I'd been in the service. He was unimpressed hearing that although I'd been in the army, I hadn't seen combat. He asked what I did for a living. Hearing that I was a psychologist, he kept digging but as an aside said, "Yeah, my wife is one. If you're dreaming about apples, they tell you you're dreaming about oranges."

I commiserated with him, "Yes, people are quick to tell us what our dreams mean even if they don't have a clue that dreams are unique to every individual."

Without words, he looked up from his digging with an expression that said he was in full agreement. Full agreement, however, didn't mean that he was at all interested in sharing any of his dreams with a psychologist, even in a casual way. He had probably decided that the temporary comfort found in a bar was easier than going for professional help.

It's a common assumption that anyone with even one deployment in Iraq or Afghanistan can be diagnosed with posttraumatic stress disorder. I wondered if he was having the repetitive nightmares that are often an emotionally painful part of the condition. I risked invading his privacy by asking him about them.

He may also have shared his dreams all too often only to hear interpretations from overly enthusiastic listeners who thought they knew exactly what the dreams meant. Such interpretations can seem as illogical to the dreamer as changing the apples that represent the dreamer's interpretation to oranges, which represent the listener's interpretation.

Even if a listener's interpretation makes some kind of logical sense, the additional information is a burdensome intrusion that can make the dreamer's work even more complicated. And he sure wasn't going to take a chance by telling his dreams to a vet who hadn't seen combat. He probably shared a popular assumption that a situation can't be understood unless the person listening has undergone the same thing. I suspect that even if I had seen combat his fear of bringing the nightmares to consciousness would probably have prompted him to say that the combat I had seen was different so I still wouldn't understand.

We hadn't connected in the way I had hoped. The chance of having a combat vet, who was a complete stranger, open up to me about traumatic combat experiences was very slim. Ideally, he wouldn't have been digging in a hole with me standing next to him on the dirt; he would have been in my office where he could have given me enough information to determine what kind of professional help, if any, he had obtained. With that knowledge, I would have been able to provide some information about treatments designed specifically for those suffering from PTSD.

There has been a great deal of progress in developing cognitive and somatic approaches to dealing with the type of nightmares encountered by those with PTSD. Experts in the field know that PTSD sufferers have nightmares that are unlike more common nightmares that can be labeled as weird, bizarre, or at least unusual. Those with PTSD have a type of nightmare that is a replication of actual traumatic events and is seen by the dreamer as being more like a replay. Some consider PTSD nightmares not to be nightmares at all, but flashbacks that occur during sleep rather than when awake.

Making treatment more difficult is the fact that PTSD nightmares can take over much of one's dream life and rob the dreamer of the more common dreams that point to solutions for everyday problems. The result is that those with severe PTSD may not even be able to imagine the future in their waking lives.

The belief that talking about something will make it better is usually accurate. Unfortunately that idea may not always be true when working with PTSD sufferers. Ordinary suggestions to provide the repetitive nightmares with new endings can be ineffective. New treatments use a similar approach but with far more attention paid to the degree of discomfort the PTSD sufferer is in when recalling the original dream. Too little discomfort will result in no progress. Too much discomfort can result in the person being retraumatized. Treatment for PTSD requires not merely a skilled psychotherapist, but a specialist who is aware of the latest research on an approach called focusing-oriented dreamwork. The marine's careful guardedness indicates that he has not yet found such a therapist.

Having made his point regarding a discussion of nightmares allowed the marine to relax and talk about what was really on his mind. "I'm glad you're getting this pavilion but I sure wish the weather would cool down a bit. I hate digging when the sweat gets in my eyes and starts to burn." I responded that the forecast wasn't promising, but maybe when the pavilion was finished, he might enjoy coming back, having lunch inside in the shade and then going out on the lake and doing a little fishing. He smiled. We had finally connected.

FEAR AND TRAUMA

The Human Cash Register

THE HUMAN CASH REGISTER

The annual International Association for the Study of Dreams conference is a dream world extravaganza. Hundreds of people come from all over the world to meet fellow dreamers and learn the latest about dream interpretation methods, research, and other dream-related activities. My scheduled presentation of dream stories for the conference was on my mind as I pulled into the local gas station. The young attendant had an emaciated appearance that was heightened by his smooth white skin and colorless straight shoulder length hair. He paced back and forth at the pumps like a caged animal, stopping only to pump gas.

Standing next to him as he fed gas into the car, I invited conversation by telling him I was to give a presentation on dreams and wondered if he had any dreams about the gas station. His response was painful to watch. His face tightened up. "Basically I'm a human cash register waiting to be taken advantage of. My dreams are always nightmares where a guy breaks in and I get held up with a gun in my face. I've had a really busy week and there's plenty of money inside waiting to be stolen." With a sense of hopelessness, he looked down and said, "My dreams are strange." He handed me back my credit card. I volunteered that there were ways to deal with such nightmares, but he resumed his pacing, already on the alert for the next customer. Our conversation was over.

The young man's emotionally charged view of himself as a vulnerable "human cash register" will reinforce seeing himself as a victim in waking life and also encourage continued dreams of being robbed. He had demonstrated a strength in the area of visualization while describing his dreams and needs to use that strength to create a picture of himself as being safe and protected. Ideally, he would reenter the dream and have a conversation with the bad guys that would reveal what in his life is prompting his fears. Regardless of the approach he uses, it will be important for him to avoid killing the imagined bad guys. The bad guys in dreams who have been killed usually come back from the dead in a later dream, more powerful and fearsome than ever. If they don't, equally terrorizing substitutes can be expected to take their place.

Visualizations of successful dream outcomes can be beneficial not only by reducing nightmares, but by their calming and stress-reducing effect. Research indicates that we experience the same physiological responses while thinking about something as we do when we are actually participating in the event. Over the long term, positive creative visualizations send messages of strength to our unconscious. The gas station attendant has the ability to replace his victim mentality and become a stronger, less fearful individual ready to confront future life challenges. There's also no reason why the young gas station attendant can't continue to see himself as a human cash register, let's just hope he'll choose to be a safe and protected one.

THE RATS

Over the years, I'd given numerous evening dream presentations at a nearby tearoom. I dropped by one afternoon when business was slow. The owner and I sat down and enjoyed some tea and scones. Eventually we got to the topic of dreams and my practice of dream gathering. She suggested I talk with Jodie, her new assistant. "Jodie has really scary dreams."

On my next visit, I got a chance to talk with Jodie, an apparently competent hard worker whose discerning gaze conveyed the impression of intelligence and a keen mind. I asked her about her dreams. Hesitating slightly and with an air of resignation she said, "All my dreams are annoying and nonstop. There's one that keeps coming back."

There are rats all around me. They're like a plague.

My questioning look brought out her interpretation. "There are rats; you know, the rats represent people in my life. The whole thing is probably phobic. I think it's due to subliminal feelings of helplessness. I think it's situational. I'm reacting to other people's behavior. If they feel bad, I feel bad. I use thought blocking and try to have pleasant thoughts. I've gotten into better sleep practices. I sleep in all cotton items. I also think that diet has a lot to do with it. I drink valerian tea prior to going to bed. I surround myself with positive people. I hate negativity!"

I offered Jodie the possibility of working with the dream by engaging the rats in a dialogue in order to begin shedding some light on the unwanted negativity in her life. Her answer was razor sharp, "No, it's too frightening." Jodie was content with her dream interpretation and the positive life changes she had made.

Indicating no interest in pursuing the matter further, she switched the conversation to a personal question about ending a lifelong friendship with a person whom she viewed as becoming increasingly negative. Jodie's friend had shared a dream series with her that was much like Jodie's rat dreams, but with monsters taking the place of the rats. A difference was that one of the monsters showed up with the face of the dreamer, Jodie's friend. At the thought of her friend's face being on the monster, Jodie stopped talking as if she had been about to enter the forbidden room of Bluebeard's castle. It was safer to retreat into a discussion about the weather than to consider the underlying possibility that her face could show up on a rat.

Nevertheless, our conversation continued whenever I dropped by for tea. Jodie routinely considered external causes and reasons for her recurring bad dreams. She avoided any serious consideration of how her own personal history and personality could be important factors in attracting rats.

Jodie's realization that she might one day see her face on one of the rats must have been terrifying. She had been working for years to avoid people who in any way might suggest negativity. She must know that to see her face on a rat would be proof that the negativity had overtaken her as well as her friend. What she has been unaware of or chose to ignore was the fact that we draw to ourselves whatever we focus on. By putting so much personal attention on negativity for so long, she had set the stage for it to envelop her.

Also, we don't know what might have initially triggered her fear of negativity. It may well have been an abusive parent, sibling, or caretaker. In such cases, people unconsciously surround themselves with similar people as if in a bad dream in order to have the opportunity to understand from a position of strength what had been so devastating in earlier, sometimes formative, years.

Jodie's friend, rather than being someone to avoid, is someone who is presenting an opportunity for growth. Jodie has an opportunity to come to a more mature conscious understanding of negativity and help heal her fear of what negativity represents. By gathering the courage, Jodie could take her friend into confidence and discuss negativity, having her friend's dream as a starting place. Over time, both friends would have the opportunity to grow in resolving their personal fears. Jodie would no longer need to waste so much energy in avoiding the people she considers to be negative. Having become more positive herself, she would no longer have to make conscious attempts at surrounding herself with positive people; they would just show up as a reflection of herself.

Sometime later, during one of my regular visits to the tearoom, Jodie's story came to mind. Asking if the rat dreams were continuing, she said yes. It was near the end of her shift, but she took the time to hurriedly say that she needed to be satisfied with what life had given her. At the same time, beads of perspiration emerging on her forehead emphasized a look of resolution that said, "I'm going to continue facing those rats and as scary as they are, I'm not going to let them have their way with me."

Not wanting to be added to the list of rats in her life, I chose not to offer any other suggestions. Wishing her the best, I silently blew her a heartfelt kiss as she turned to go.

BUDDY'S DREAMS

Woods Lake in Warren County, New Jersey, was a hot spot in the 1950s. People would come from all over to rent the rowboats and sailboats, or just take advantage of its two beaches. A small roller rink and playground helped to make it the perfect family getaway. There were even a couple of restaurants that offered a touch of nightlife. Easier access to the Jersey shore with its boardwalks and amusement parks left Woods Lake deserted except for the residents of the small community in which the homes were mostly converted summer cottages. The current residents are caring folks who act like they stepped out of *It's A Wonderful Life*, the sentimental 1946 film starring Jimmy Stewart.

The road surrounding the lake is ideal for leisurely spring and summer walks. On one of my afternoon walks, the sound of the local bullfrog was interrupted with a loud call. "Hey, you retired yet?" Looking back, there was Buddy giving me a grin. The first time he had called to me was at dusk one evening when he handed me an old reflective orange colored vest, one of several he had put aside for late-night walkers. "You'll need that when you walk in the evening so you don't get run over." It was good enough advice and that old vest has gotten a lot of use. Buddy's grin dissolved into a thoughtful expression as he spoke about his difficulties in adjusting to his own retirement. "You don't know what you're gonna do." He went on to talk about catching up on projects around the house before becoming more serious.

Buddy looked as if he were going to talk more about his struggle with cancer that I'd heard about on previous walks. Instead, he described a large New York City medical center that he was going to the following week for a cochlear implant. Although many Vietnam vets are reluctant to discuss their experiences, Buddy had shared some of his, this time explaining that he had only 8 percent of his hearing in one ear due to a bunker explosion. "Yeah, horseshoes and hand grenades can do a lot of damage when they're real close. I wouldn't be here if I hadn't been wearing my flak jacket." His appreciation for that protective vest must have been related to his interest in protecting walkers by providing them with safety vests.

There is little doubt that Buddy is still dealing with posttraumatic stress. He is probably having repeating nightmares that don't change, in contrast to the changing nightmares of those without posttraumatic stress. Flashbacks and nightmares can last for decades, are often lifelong, and can become even more distressing after retirement in the absence of job-related distractions.

Hoping that Buddy would share a dream that could provide a clue as to how he might reduce his stress, I told him that I was spending some of my time teaching people about dreams and wondered if he might share something based on his experience.

There was no doubt that Buddy could contribute to the understanding of dreams. He started slowly, "Nobody knows everything about dreams, but there sure is a subconscious. Stuff pops up that people haven't thought about in years.

"I used to have dreams that I was stark naked—nothing on. I covered myself with my hands, but nobody even noticed I was naked." Laughing, he demonstrated how he had tried to cover himself in the dream. Buddy was enjoying his discourse on dreams. "You know the best dreams? When you fly. I don't even know where I go, but I know they're the best." At that, the big man turned into an excited little boy joyfully showing me how he spreads his arms, runs a few steps, and takes off flying. But a moment later, all signs of the little boy were gone. With an expectant look at his watch, he was back in the army again. "Oh, it's time for happy hour." He waved good-bye and headed toward his house.

Buddy's dreams of being naked reflect how he must have felt in Vietnam, completely naked, exposed, and defenseless against the enemy, while getting insufficient validation of his feelings from those around him. It's no wonder that Buddy looks forward to flying dreams in which the horror and mutilations of the bunker experience are forgotten and left behind. Buddy's humor conceals the emotional pain that can never be far from the surface, that relentless pain that no flak jacket could have prevented. Vietnam vets are known for complaining less than their counterparts who fought in Iraq and Afghanistan. Now, decades later, new treatments are being developed for PTSD. We can hope that Buddy and his fellow Vietnam vets will receive the help that those new treatments can offer.

NO, I DON'T WANT TO!

Amy, the young efficient cashier at the local home supply center, had scanned my purchases and noted the accepted status of my credit card in the blink of an eye. Looking up from the cash register with direct eye contact in a practiced, speedy manner, she said, "Four digits." The words called out for me to give an immediate response.

My head spun around as I clicked on a mental file that contained numbers. There was the numerical code on the back of my credit card, but that was only three digits. The last four digits of my home phone number took its place. Then the unlikely possibility that the number she wanted was the additional four numbers added to my five-digit zip code produced a mental haze. Seeing my confusion, she indulged me with a smile as she clarified her request saying, "Last four of your credit card."

With the problem solved and the development of what seemed like instant rapport, I popped the question, "Do you ever dream about this place?" I just knew I was going to hear a good dream. Her reply came with continued digital speed. "No, I don't want to; I work thirty-five hours a week." She was already looking at the next person in line.

When it comes to dreams, people often avoid answering questions about their dream life initially, but then quickly go on to tell their life history. In this case, I'd hit a dead end.

On my way out, if I'd thrown Amy a quick look, I might have been caught in the act and seen her giving me an equally quick look of frustration that would have said, "I'm sorry, I've been there, I've done that. I can't do it. Life is too hard right now."

Amy's comment about work was a reminder that even when dream interpretation is lightheartedly referred to as dream play, it is still work. At a superficial level it may appear quick and easy to go to sleep with a question and get up with an answer in the morning. But to the contrary, useful dream interpretation includes several steps.

First, the intention to recall dreams must be set. Next, the dreamer must write down or record what is recalled. Finally, there needs to be a search for meaning. This last step includes the frequently ignored necessity of making a life change either in action or thought. And making life changes in meaningful ways requires energy, creativity, and perseverance. And that's not easy work.

FAST FOOD IS A KILLER

My next-door neighbor Ellie was a cute, petite seventeen-year-old high school student with a sparkle and zest for living that you could see a mile away—a real dynamo. She knew I was a dream specialist and asked me to give a presentation on dreams to her health class as part of an assignment she was doing with her best friend Danielle. I was glad to do it and asked Ellie and Danielle to share dreams with me in return.

After the presentation, Ellie looked at me with her characteristic glow and said, "Here's my dream."

I got a cheeseburger, but there was a gun inside it. A guy comes up, reaches into the cheeseburger, grabs the gun and aims it at me. I'm scared and run down an alley as he's shooting at me. I lie down on the ground hoping he'll think he got me.

Without a pause she continued, giving an interpretation as if it were simply part of the dream. "Fast food is my favorite food: KFC, McDonald's, and Wendy's. The dream was telling me that fast food is going to kill me. Get it?"

Her effervescent smile coming with the enthusiasm of the "aha" moment and belief of having interpreted her dream correctly prevented me from doing any on the spot questioning. I didn't want to dash her delightfully contagious high. But that richly rewarding and exciting moment of insight within dreamwork doesn't signal an end—it's a beginning. In this case, the realization was a signal to reflect on just how fast foods were going to be the killer. Was it a reference to her allowance, digestion, complexion, or possibly her weight?

Ellie graduated and went off to college. I didn't see her for a couple of years. When I did see her, I was shocked. She wasn't the petite little girl she had been. In fact, she was quite big.

Seeing her reminded me of her dream and her interpretation that fast food was a killer. I wondered if the reference had been to her weight, which would certainly have been likely for a teenager. If so, Ellie had probably treated her dream as a story, coming to a conclusion about its meaning, and then allowing it to be forgotten. In fact, when in the course of our conversation I mentioned the dream, Ellie drew a blank. By virtually ignoring the dream, she had omitted the most important part of dream interpretation, that of taking action.

By addressing such questions, she would have been able to make changes in her fast-food eating habits that would allow her to "live." It's likely that subsequent dreams would have revealed that she didn't need to fear the guy with the gun in the first place, that he didn't want to kill her, but that shooting at her was the best way to warn her that she was putting herself in danger by eating so much fast food.

RELIGION AND SPIRITUALITY

You Can't Judge a Book by its Cover

Arthur Strock, Ph.D.

YOU CAN'T JUDGE A BOOK BY ITS COVER

It was an oppressively hot, humid afternoon that only New Jersey summers and the South American rainforests can produce. A huge backhoe had turned much of my backyard into a deep hole with a tall mound of fresh soil and boulders next to it. The machine operator was shaping the hole to fit a new septic tank. His trademark of being calm showed as he managed the levers that moved the bucket as easily as moving a spoon through custard. Suddenly silence replaced the unmuffled sound of the backhoe and the bucket stopped abruptly. Ray eased himself out of the cab, but pain showed in his voice. "The bucket's cracked."

Ray pulled out his cell phone, and within half an hour, a tired-looking and rusted-out pickup truck showed up by the side yard. The driver, a welder with a two-day stubble, wore ragged clothing that matched the look of his truck. He greeted the machine operator and examined the cracked bucket. After working out a plan, the two old fishing buddies sat down and reminisced about the trips they'd taken as if they were at a school reunion, seeing each other for the first time in years.

Sitting next to them, I felt like a guest at a private party. The old man spoke eloquently of fishing locations in the far north that allowed me to imagine the smell of clean fresh air, the beautiful greens and browns of wilderness terrain, and the sparkle and gurgle of pristine streams. The mystical quality of his stories led me to ask him about his dreams.

Saying nothing, the old man pulled out a dirty wallet and found a couple of worn, grease stained pieces of notebook paper that were torn and starting to disintegrate like a much used roadmap. Carefully unfolding them, he handed them to me.

Early Morning 5-4-07 <u>I Dreamed Jesus was Coming from the Heavens to the Earth</u> *by Dan Walker.*

I, Dan Walker, had the most VIVID insightful dream of all my years. I do remember the exact clear details AND the emotion that flooded my total senses.

I was by myself, driving through open country with gentle rolling hills punctuated with farm pasture, barns, barbed wire fences, and occasional small ponds. The beautiful weather, blue skies, and wild flowers in full bloom made travel very pleasant.

Far in the distance were giant mountains, like the Rockies when viewed from the Great Plains. The road was paved and very smooth. There were no other vehicles to be seen until I crested a small hill. Then, there were more vehicles and people to be seen everywhere, maybe thousands. All of the people were looking into the sky and smiling, but not saying a word. I got out of my truck and scanned the sky, but not seeing anything, I turned to look at the people more closely. They ranged from infants to very old people. They were clothed differently, some in pressed suits, some in rags, but they all had a similar, most genuine gentle smile on their faces. As if on cue, all the people pivoted on their heels and fell slowly backwards, stopping at about a 45-degree angle to the ground. Then their smiles became illuminated with an all-enveloping happiness that flowed out from them, enveloping the entire space.

Finally, I walked into the midst of all these people—all of them held up, balanced by an unseen force, all of them smiling that peaceful smile. I walked up to a middle-aged person. He had farmer clothes on, a three-or four-day beard, suspenders holding up his dirty Wrangler pants. Just as I began to ask him what was happening, as if on cue again, everyone raised both hands to the sky. Their smiles projected the perfection of beauty as tears glistening in the sunlight rolled down their cheeks.

"What's going on?" I asked.

The farmer slowly moved his head and as we made eye contact, he replied, "Jesus. Jesus has come back. Don't you see him?"

I answered "NO."

His smile faded as He asked me, "Do you believe in Jesus?"

I answered, "Yes-Yes-Yes I do." At that very instant there was a sound, a very low pitch, sort of like a bubbly popping inwards or backwards. At the same instant, the whole sky got brighter than a hundred suns, and was held in place by the most gentle sensation of love that I've ever experienced. In that same instant time stood still and I was overwhelmed by what happened. I could see over the horizon and in all directions at once. The sight was incredibly impossible. I actually saw everywhere around the world at once multiplied with the sky. In the middle, wherever that was, was a most blaring intense circle of light in the midst of the intense hundred sun bright sky. I WAS IN AWE. I remember feeling so peaceful that Jesus was coming back for Me. I wasn't afraid.

I remember shouting, "WOW, WOW, and as the tears were flowing from my eyes from joy, happiness, fulfillment, contentment, I called out, "I'm here Jesus. I'm ready."

I looked up from the grease-stained paper. The dirt, grime, and ragged clothing of the man all but disappeared. Here was a man who was filled with love. Dan brought me back to the here and now by explaining that he continued to look forward to sharing the dream with anyone who showed an interest.

The dream had all the characteristics of what is called a great dream. The dream itself was visually immaculate and clear, better than a Blu-ray player could produce and it was life changing. Dan needed no dream interpretation. The dream had already done its work. He was at peace with himself and the world.

Dan had literally seen the Light, a light he had described as a soothing light brighter than a hundred suns, a light that left him in awe as he saw everywhere at the same time. He was also left with feelings of safety and peace that were beyond what he could find words to describe, let alone understand.

At first glance, the welder looked worn out. There was nothing in his outward appearance that suggested an inner vitality, a spiritual depth, or commitment to his fellow man. In fact, the question would arise from anyone looking at Dan why a good-looking, skilled machine operator like Ray would choose to get help from a person who looked like a last choice. The welder looked like the kind of person we unconsciously don't even see, much the way we might miss a book with an unappealing cover that later falls off the bookstore shelf into our hands and contains just the information we've been looking for.

TWO NUNS

Dr. O'Connor is an ophthalmologist with a delightful personality. He runs his office efficiently and has a respect for his patients' time. When I arrived for my appointment, there was only a two-minute wait before I was ushered into the examining room where an associate updated my medical history. After the update, the routine involved moving to an adjacent waiting room prior to meeting with the doctor. As I took my seat, two nuns in full black habit entered the archway to the room. One was stooped over, as she silently shuffled into the room using barely perceptible steps with the assistance of a second nun who needed to steady herself with a cane.

The two nuns were a study in light and dark. The first, with a hard, deeply etched face of weathered granite, seemed clouded in grey, lacking the energy even to sustain herself. The other, with a glowing, colorful face, radiated joy and energy to those around her. Once the two were settled in their chairs, my attention returned to a magazine only to hear a clear-voiced "Happy Easter" float into the room. The greeting came with a big smile from the nun with the cane. The half-dozen people in the room responded with everything from a surprised grunt to an enthusiastic thank you.

My mind took on a life of its own and playfully translated the "Happy Easter" into an invitation to share dreams. Rationally that was quite a stretch. But by the time my rational mind took over,

I had already crossed the room and was telling the nun about my writing and asking her if she ever had dreams of Jesus.

Her smile continued, "Yes, yes." Not wanting to be overly blunt in asking her to share one of those dreams, I shared one of my own that included Jesus, hoping that my openness would encourage her to share a dream in return. Seemingly more accustomed to listening than divulging her own personal information, the nun's head twitched ever so slightly in surprise while deciding to honor my request. She slowly explained that she was from an area in Mexico that had many earthquakes that she called "tremblings." She then told the following dream.

The earth was trembling. There were many people standing. They all began falling down, but the Blessed Virgin Mary remained standing. She is the intercessor you know.

The nun's dream reminded me of a conversation about Mother Mary that my neighbor and I had years before. Although my neighbor was not Catholic and rarely went to church, she reported that her son, who had passed, told her in a dream that Mary was called upon very little for help. He urged his mother to call upon Mary if she was ever in need.

I then shared what my neighbor had said, to which the nun showed no surprise. A silence followed, much like the pause that occurs between tracks on a CD. The silence was broken abruptly by the nurse announcing my name from across the room. She didn't need to add that it was my turn to see the doctor. The nun acknowledged my look of apology at being unable to continue our conversation.

Following the examination, I looked back into the waiting room. The two nuns were still there, the one frozen in time; her companion resting with her head tilted back, eyes closed. She may have been reliving her vision of the Blessed Virgin Mary, possibly gaining strength from the dream to continue helping her companion stay upright and keep from falling. Whatever the case, it would not have been fair to interrupt the nun's reverie.

The nun had shared a dream of Mary, not Jesus. Would a dream of Jesus have been too deeply personal for her to share? Or does she just have a closer connection with the Blessed Virgin? It might be that the dream of the earthquake was just the first dream of a series that came to mind about Mother Mary's continuing role on Earth.

Whatever the reason, as so often happens with spontaneous dream sharing, the experience was much like seeing the tip of the iceberg. There is so much lying unseen below the surface.

JESUS, SATAN, AND ISIS

The view of the new carefully tended red brick Middleton School of the Redeemer was framed naturally by the beautifully manicured grounds on which it stood. The children, happily at play during recess, stood out against the background of green grass, blue skies, and billowy white clouds. Inside, Mrs. Roberts, the school administrator, was as efficient as ever, welcoming me and sending for the student who was being considered for extra reading help.

The girl smiled the genuine, open, easy smile of the typically friendly ten-year-old. The school library was the perfect place for ability testing, with its large windows and welcoming sunlight. The testing was accomplished easily, after which Chrissie and I chatted. She expressed concern about her reading ability, which was in keeping with the teacher's concern for this girl who was described as a joy to have in class: hard working and eager to please. Chrissie also spoke about how she loved to draw. I asked if she ever drew her dreams. She said no, she hadn't, but that she did have dreams and they were really scary.

One time there was an angel up in heaven talking to me, telling me, "You have to come before the ISIS comes." The clouds were getting all grey and closing up. I fell backward and hit my head. When I woke up there were a dozen people trying to kill me and this Chinese teacher stabbed me in the heart and people were laughing when he cut my head off. Then angels came and they fought the people by punching them. It felt like the angels had magic and Jesus took his one-sided gold sword and cut through the leader of the bad people. Jesus' favorite angel was Johnson and he gave his sword to Johnson, but Johnson's name came up on the sword in black letters. Satan came down and took the sword from Johnson and beat Johnson with it. Then Jesus came and cut Satan's head off.

"I woke up and cried for my mom and she came into my room. She told me it was just a dream and that everything would be okay. After she left, I went back to sleep. I didn't want to, but I went back into the dream and finished it."

Jesus was on the cross with his crown and dirty robe. People let the other two guys off their crosses. Those two guys beat Jesus and then took him off the cross. Johnson, the angel, took the sword and put it through Jesus' belly button. Jesus was in pain and yelled, "Stop it." Then Jesus flew up, took Johnson with him and told him, "You're home." Rain was coming down red blood. Johnson wanted to be in charge like Satan.

Chrissie took hold of the red cross hanging on a chain around her neck as the bell rang. The period was over.

Walking Chrissie back to class, a boy's voice cut through the din and commotion of the students changing classes, "I had a dream—something about my family." Noise from the hallway drowned out any further explanation. Hopefully the boy's dream wasn't as horrifying as the nightmare I had just heard.

Chrissie's smiles and age-appropriate behavior had concealed grave fears of death and poor school performance. Her nightmare brought those fears to the surface in a forbidding mix of confusion. Individuals from Biblical times interacted with individuals from the present time. Individuals were strong one minute and weak the next. Making the situation even more confusing was that no one in the dream was safe to be with. Individuals switched with lightning speed from being good one moment to bad the next.

The nightmare was very likely prompted by exposure to Biblical stories not adapted for children and adult news programs. Jesus, Satan, and the archangel Michael are clearly referenced in the Bible. Secretary of Homeland Security Jeh Johnson and the Middle East terrorist group ISIS had recently been in the news. Both the archangel Michael and members of ISIS are often pictured holding swords. ISIS is known for beheading hostages with swords. But who was the Chinese teacher who stabbed Chrissie in the heart and then cut off her head while people laughed? And why was Chrissie so traumatically impacted by the Bible and news media stories?

Unfortunately, many people attempt to explain away nightmares by saying that they are simply replays of events seen and heard on the news. If such were the case, almost everyone watching or listening to the news on a daily basis would be having nightmares. Reasons for nightmares are numerous. They include physical factors such as illness, food intake, and drugs; as well as emotional factors including stress and traumatic life incidents. Nightmares are a call to deal with such underlying causes.

Nightmare activity in children can be reduced by shielding them from R-rated stories, whether from the Bible or the news media. For Chrissie, however, much time will need to be spent with her in order to help determine possible underlying physical and emotional causes. She will need to be provided with ways to work through her waking-life fears that have been heightened by the media. Such fears, whether unconscious or conscious, are sapping Chrissie's energy that could be used to better advantage during school learning activities and play.

As terrifying as Chrissie's dream was, it may actually only hint at deeper issues. If Chrissie's nightmares continue, she will need professional help. Chrissie will need far more than reassurance that everything will be okay. In fact, anyone giving Chrissie such reassurance will lose credibility because Chrissie experienced the nightmare as real. Parents can start by shielding Chrissie from graphic Bible stories and media news programs. Bible lessons will need to be retaught. Parents could profit from meeting with Chrissie's teacher in an attempt to determine what the Chinese teacher symbolizes for Chrissie. And because Chrissie loves to draw, she will be able to begin healing work through her own art and other forms of therapy. With ongoing help, Chrissie's smile will change from being a socially acceptable but misleading way of presenting herself to a more accurate representation of how she really feels.

THE CENTRAL FIGURE OF OUR DREAMS

The day was so pleasant, a perfect day to enjoy lunch at an outdoor café. The old man alone at a small table welcomed my request to join him and was soon talking about how time seemed to be speeding up and that his life would sooner rather than later come to a close. He was still working. He had enough money and didn't need to work, but working was a part of him. At the same time, he was acutely aware that his reason for existence for over half a century had been his job and that interest was dying. He needed to know if his new-found passion for working directly with people to help improve their lives was genuinely felt and would be reason enough to leave his old job or was merely a good excuse for feeling tired enough to leave the job. His thoughts floated on a mist of memories and moved into telling me a dream.

A slender, almost shapeless woman covered in silence appeared before me; her features dissolved before the sheen and smooth perfection of her short silvery-white hair. I was totally focused on the woman. She was my comfort, my source of reassurance that I needed to give energy to a new life. She could release me from my worries that as an old man I no longer had the potential to make a mark in the world, a new world of speeding change that disappears ahead of my comprehension.

Time was visibly absent. Neither I nor the woman disturbed the stillness. We just stood opposite each other, seeing each other, but with no exchange of any kind.

We usually consider beings such as the woman in the old man's dream as the most important figure in our dreams. Who we draw into our dreams as guides and helpers is influenced by the depth of our problems, our belief system, our intentions for direction in life, and unconscious drives.

In the old man's case, a heavenly angelic being appeared. This being with her unspoken power and beauty seemed to shift the attention away from the old man. He seemed to become only a bystander. Nevertheless, it is the old man who is the focal point of the dream. The old man in the dream is much like a patient on the operating table of a teaching hospital's large surgical amphitheater. The surgeon, like the archetypical figure in the old man's dream, is critically important, but is there only to serve and heal the patient.

Such dreams in all of their quiet, veiled power come to celebrate us as half-asleep dreamers, who when awake, can be enormously vital and important contributors to the welfare of humanity. The old man's dream had been comforting and had given him a sense of reassurance that using his energy for more service-oriented work would finally allow him to enjoy the sense of fulfillment that comes with making a positive and meaningful difference in the world.

I see him moving through old age: leaving his old job, pursuing his passion, and beginning a new life as a much happier individual.

HARVARD SQUARE

At the recommendation of a friend, I'd gone to Harvard Square in Cambridge, Massachusetts, for the express purpose of collecting dreams. The day was picture perfect with clear skies and the comfort of a light summer breeze. The only people there were three dangerous-looking young adults with a surprisingly calm-looking black dog, sitting together on the grass. They looked like misplaced California hippies from the 1960s who had lost their desire for peace and love.

They wouldn't have been my first choice to ask about dreams if anyone else had been there. As I approached them, they ignored me until I reached out to pet the dog while making small talk about the weather. When I asked the group if I could join them, they nodded indifferently, and continued passing around the stub of a very battered-looking small cigar.

After what seemed like a long time, there was no indication that I would be welcomed into their conversation. Not knowing how they would respond, I self-consciously announced that I was collecting dreams for a book, and asked if they had any interesting ones they could share.

The cleanest-looking member of the group, with a feather sticking upright in his curly, blond hair, stated defiantly that he didn't want to remember his dreams. He thought they would make his life more complicated than it already was.

The man sitting to my right, who I later learned was called Chaser, was talking to the woman across from him. He had a deathly looking pale complexion; closely shaved head; rings in his mouth, nose and ears; and a faded tattoo on his chest. He heard my question and switched topics in mid-sentence. He began telling the woman about a dream his friend Mike had; in a voice that was intended for me to hear.

Chaser's excitement in describing the dream was reflected in his quick speech pattern, rapidly shifting gaze, and increasingly restless body movements; all of which added a hyper quality to his appearance. Chaser shifted his attention to me, allowing the other group members to fade into the background and immerse themselves in a discussion of their contempt for the injustices of the world.

In spite of his gaunt appearance, Chaser had a sincere look of admiration as he explained that his long-time friend Mike frequently remembered dreams and had even started going to church. Mike had dreamt of Chaser and in the dream had given him a prescription for Adderall. Mike told Chaser that he hoped the prescription would help him slow down and become more relaxed—less uptight.

Chaser's friends began sharing a new joint. He looked away, indicating that he would pass, and continued talking, "I don't know if Adderall would be for me, but Mike has his head screwed on straight. I used to be a drug addict," and as if to emphasize his point, he added, "I even had a needle plunged into my heart in an emergency room to save my life after an overdose."

As my attention returned to Chaser, I could feel the draw of his urgency to find help even from me, a complete stranger. Injecting medication straight into the heart muscle is now considered an outdated resuscitation treatment; it is more likely that Chaser dreamt this scenario than experienced it in an emergency room.

Other members of the group were oblivious to our conversation. Against the backdrop of the group members' murmurings I got a chance to give him some sincere advice, "Hey Chaser, I know you don't trust the whole medical establishment, but you can't keep going on the way you are. You'll do yourself in. Why not go see a doctor? Take Mike along with you so you can see if the doctor makes sense." Chaser heard me, but made no commitment to taking my advice. I thanked him for his trust and for being so open with me.

As we meet others and share dreams, we make unexpectedly deep and meaningful connections. It was no coincidence that I entered the lives of these young people the morning after Chaser was given a dream message about his drug use. My presence as a listener allowed Chaser to talk about his friend's dream and its reference to his high anxiety level and hyperactivity. In the dream Mike shared with Chaser, the reference to Adderall may have been a way to offer support for his friend to look into taking a prescription drug for his ADD.

As I walked away from Chaser that day, I reflected on the power of our dreams and how they guide and enhance our efforts to improve our lives. Chaser is fortunate to have a friend like Mike who can provide him with much needed council toward creating a safer and more satisfying life. It's time now for Chaser to take the next step into that new life.

VISITATIONS

The Barber's Mom

THE BARBER'S MOM

It was a hot summer day. A street improvement project had blocked easy access to the barbershop. The shop was almost empty. Jenny was free and got right to work. She's a delightful woman who is sincerely interested in her customers. As usual, she asked about my family, and being interested in dreams herself, asked if I ever had dreams about family members. Hearing that I had, she called to her fellow barber who was busy dying her hair at the back of the shop. "Kitty, you want to find out what that dream of yours means?" Straightening up, Kitty almost knocked the hair coloring jars from the edge of the sink. Saying nothing, she stepped over to my chair with the first full smile on her face I could recall seeing in all my visits.

Her eyes then took on a distant look as she described a series of dreams in which she saw her mom in a coffin. "My mom rises up out of her body like a spirit or something. Then she talks, but I don't remember what she talks about. Then she says, 'I gotta go now.'" With hand gestures, Kitty showed how her mother lies back down in space and slowly sinks into her body.

She sadly spoke of the months she had spent at her mother's bedside, wanting desperately to be there when her mother died. She seemed unaware that some of her hair dye was dripping on the floor. She spoke of how she would leave her mom's bedroom only for short periods of time to get something to eat. In remembering what had taken place, Kitty's feelings of frustration resurfaced. "My mom died when I was in the kitchen. My sister was at home too and could have called to me. I was just thirty seconds away." Then with a return of focus to her dreams, she continued, "My sister thinks my dreams are weird and wants to know why I don't have normal dreams like hers, where Mom is cooking or sitting in her chair or doing stuff around the house. I wonder too. I tell her that I don't know why. Maybe my dreams have something to do with the fact that I wasn't there with Mom when she died and missed her saying good-bye or something."

I mentioned that it was a shame she didn't recall what her mother was saying in the dreams, which might have helped answer her questions. My comment was seemingly ignored as Kitty said that her eight-year-old niece had seen Nana one night after she died and was upset that Nana disappeared when she went to give her a hug.

Kitty returned to the sink at the back of the shop to finish dying her hair. My barber finished up quietly. Rather than leave immediately, I sat down in the waiting area and began writing down what Kitty had told me. The shop had started to fill up and Kitty was soon cutting another customer's hair. Blurred bits and pieces of conversations provided the isolation I needed to continue writing.

Kitty's voice drifted through the fog and looking up I saw her hovering over me. She spoke confidentially in a hushed voice as if needing to be sure I understood something very important. "In one of the dreams, Mom was lying down in her bed at home where she died. She rose up out of her body and was talking to me. When people started coming into the house to express their condolences, she put her finger to her mouth and said, 'Shh, be quiet, I gotta go lie down and pretend I'm dead because they think I am.'" Without waiting for a reply, Kitty went back to cutting her customer's hair.

Fortunately I had stayed in the shop to record Kitty's dream or I would have missed hearing the key to understanding why Kitty was having dreams that were different from her sister's. Kitty's sister apparently had no questions about her mother's death. Her dreams were unrelated to what happens to a person after death. Kitty's dreams, on the other hand, were frightening and confusing dreams of her mother dying again and again. In a way that Kitty did not accept, her wish to be with her mother at the time of death was coming true night after night in her dreams. Being with her mother in the dream state when her mother died, however, had not allowed Kitty to release her disappointment.

Kitty could recall only one dream in which she remembered what her mother had said. Her mother's lighthearted humor at shushing her daughter with a secret that she wasn't dead was upsetting and still on the fringe of Kitty's comprehension. It took courage for Kitty to reveal that message from her mother. The message challenged Kitty's belief about life after death. Kitty is guarded about her belief that her mother is in fact alive in spirit, even though her niece's experience adds credibility to that belief. When Kitty finally accepts that there is life after death, the disappointment and possibly guilt that she feels at not being with her mother at the time of physical death will gradually disappear. After all, her mother's message was very clear: she isn't dead, people just think she is.

Arthur Strock, Ph.D.

GINO'S MOTHER-IN-LAW

It's always a treat going to the Town Square Barber Shop, a fourth-generation family business that recently won a Best Barbershop in New Jersey award. After arriving from Italy in 1929, Dominic opened the business and was soon joined by his son-in-law, Angelo. On a recent visit, Angelo, now in his eighties, was busy at the first chair. His son, Gino, was free and invited me to sit down. Having known me for years, Gino felt comfortable sharing personal information, this time about the strange electrical things that began happening in his house after his mother-in-law died.

Gino told me that recently his wife plugged the vacuum cleaner into an outlet in the spare bedroom, but the vacuum wouldn't turn on. Gino checked the circuit breaker, but it hadn't been tripped. Whenever he plugged in the vacuum, it worked fine. The second time it happened, Gino checked the outlet with a circuit tester. It was in perfect working order. After the third time, he became concerned about the possibility of short circuits and fire hazards. He called an electrician who spent the better part of a day examining wiring throughout the entire house, but found no problems. Gino said that at the same time they were experiencing electrical problems, his usually quiet dog positioned himself in the doorway to the dining room every night at the same time and began barking. The family couldn't see anything to bark at.

Knowing I was interested in dreams, Gino told me a dream he had about his mother-in-law's brothers at the same time the strange things were happening in his house. He made a point of explaining that one of the brothers was alive and one was dead. In his dream, the dead brother was faceless, but recognizable by his clothing and body build. In the dream, Gino witnessed the dead brother scolding the brother who was still alive and jabbing him in the shoulder saying, "You're still doing it; you're still doing it. You've got to stop!"

Gino's face was suddenly a blur right next to mine, his hand held up as if he were in court taking an oath, "I swear on my mother's grave this is all true!"

Startled, I mumbled, "I believe you," and asked if the brother who was still alive was a drinker.

That was all Gino needed to hear. "Yes! Hiding bottles in the house, beating his wife, leaving home, sobering up, and then coming back home to drink again." Gino became silent as he finished my haircut.

In order to help solve the mystery involving the dog's barking, the electrical problems, and his dream, Gino could experiment by initiating dreams to contact his mother-in-law for answers. He could also talk to her out loud whenever the dog did his unexplainable barking and be open to unexpected outcomes. Even without additional information, however, the close relationships among Gino's family members, as well as the dog, support the idea of a comprehensive unspoken family-based plan to help one another both on this plane of existence and from the so-called other side.

Assuming there was an unspoken family plan to help the mother-in-law's brother deal with his problem drinking, the family had some unfinished business to attend to. The brother on the other side can't get through to his brother on this side because alcohol consumption interferes with dreaming. Gino's dream channel is open. Because he has had dreams of both brothers that were linked in time to his mother-in-law's passing, he seems to have been chosen as the family member best able to relay a stop-drinking message to the brother still on this plane.

It would be very easy for Gino to become so absorbed as an observer of the paranormal events that have occurred that he doesn't realize his role in the plan. If he fails to do his part, relaying the message to his mother-in-law's brother to stop drinking, there's no telling what Gino's mother-in-law may be up to next, but it's sure to be more than just catching the dog's attention and playing around with an electrical outlet.

THE WALMART PHOTO COUNTER

Late one Sunday afternoon, I had just time enough for a quick trip to the Walmart photo counter to get a few pictures printed before doing the grocery shopping. Editing took less time than expected and the clerk's projected printout time was only fifteen minutes. So after a little shopping, I headed back to the counter. Seeing that I was in a hurry, the clerk said, "Your pictures are being processed now."

My impatient glance at the clock caught the attention of the intuitive sales clerk who began treating me with the kind of care usually reserved for a well-to-do patron at Tiffany's. With genuine warmth and understanding, she took the time to explain in detail just why the printing was taking longer than expected. It was quiet at the counter. There was nothing to provide a distraction from having to wait. So why not bring up the topic of dreams?

"Are you a dreamer? I mean do you recall your dreams? I'm writing a book on dreams."

The questions came out of the blue, but the clerk showed the poise of a well-to-do hostess at a party for notables. "I dream all the time. I really need to tell you this dream about my sister."

We were best friends. I always felt badly that she had a scar that ran from the side of her face all the way down her neck. She got it in the automobile accident that actually killed our grandmother. A few years ago she got sick; none of us in the family knew she was dying, but when we took her for the last doctor's appointment, he said she had only two months to live. She said she wasn't afraid, but I didn't want her to be all alone in a hospital when she died. I didn't get there in time and I felt so guilty. Later, I saw her in a dream. She had on the most beautiful fluffy white robe. I yelled at her, "Were you afraid?" She yelled back. At first I was afraid, but now I'm happy.

Cora's face lit up with enthusiasm at recalling the dream from years before. "I've got more dreams to tell you."

"Wait a minute, what about the scar?"

Her look of surprise at my question turned to one of innocence as she said, "The scar was gone." The printing machines had completed my order. As I was paying, a line of customers was forming behind me. I hurriedly thanked Cora.

"Please wait for me. There aren't many people I can share my dreams with and I have more to tell you." I apologized, but really did need to get my grocery shopping done and promised to be back.

Dream sharing in an unlikely location had uncovered a wonderful example of a visitation dream. Not only was it reassuring that Cora's sister is at ease and happy, the dream helps to answer a question about how people will look after they pass over. Like Cora's sister, people in visitation dreams usually appear to be healthy, without the disfigurements that can accompany diseases or accidents that have occurred on the physical plane.

Dream sharing had also averted one of those potentially hurtful confrontations that can occur when we're in a hurry and give more importance than is deserved to minor things we want to get done. Instead of comments that would have fueled impatience at having to wait, a focus on dreams turned waiting time into a truly meaningful meeting of hearts and a pleasant, enduring memory.

AUNT MILLIE

Carolyn was a bit distant. She made direct eye contact with a steady gaze. She gave a small smile of understanding with a slight nod of the head during conversations. She gave the impression of having accepted what had been said, but commonly avoided expressing her own thoughts and feelings. Over the ten years we had known each other as neighbors, she had alluded to "discomforting" dreams. When given offers of help, she would give an expressionless reply, "Well, I hardly ever remember details of a dream."

What a surprise to find an email from Carolyn after I had moved from the neighborhood.

My latest dream was not at all disheartening. I wanted to share it with you. I dreamed about my favorite aunt, Aunt Millie. She died last year the morning after hosting our family's Christmas party. My last memory of her was seeing her laughing and talking to a bunch of my cousins before I left the party to go to bed.

In my dream I was at a family gathering in a big open place like a fire hall. I saw Aunt Millie across the room talking and laughing. I went over to her and she turned to me, smiling, and I said to her, "Aunt Millie, I was at the Christmas party last year and you died. How come you're here?"

She chuckled and smiled at me and said, "Neat, huh?"

And that was the end of my dream. It was curious to me that Aunt Millie had such a strong presence.

What a gem of a dream, the only dream Carolyn ever shared. Carolyn had said that her dreams were discomforting and disheartening. They must have been thought of as bad dreams, the kind that are unwelcome, upsetting and intimidating, the kind that in some ways we are glad to forget. She must have been relieved to have a good dream, especially of her much loved Aunt Millie.

Dreams of this type can evoke a sense of childlike wonder, disbelief, and in Carolyn's case, curiosity. What really happened? We can be sure that Aunt Millie was not in Carolyn's dream simply by chance. In the dream, Aunt Millie was described as real—a strong presence. She had paid Carolyn a visit. The visits from deceased loved ones usually include the reassurance that they are okay, safe, alive, and that there is nothing to worry about. In this case, Carolyn was given the opportunity to laugh and have fun with her aunt, an opportunity she had missed at the party. Perhaps Aunt Millie's saying, "neat huh?" was a way of helping Carolyn to lighten up and not take life so seriously. And in this visit, she also had her affectionate Aunt Millie all to herself, without even having to share her with the cousins.

THE MESSAGE

The day was grey, but inside the podiatrist's examination room bright pictures of tropical birds and animals in their natural settings adorned the walls and provided a welcome change from the dismal weather. The podiatrist's assistant was delightful. She pressed a button and the examination chair went up so quickly it felt like a child's amusement park ride. She checked my ankle.

"How are you doing today?"

I said, "My ankle's feeling better."

"No, I mean in general."

I told her that things were going really well, that I had just met with my editor and she liked a couple of my new stories.

"What are your stories about?" she asked. Before I knew it, she was telling me about a dream her son Buddy had ten years earlier when he was just turning four.

I was walking along beside a fence. On the other side of the fence I saw Pappy. I saw Pappy!

Pappy was her son's great-grandfather, a tower of strength for the family. He had virtually raised her husband and was a favorite of Buddy's. She remembered trying to calm Buddy down after hearing the dream, saying there was no need to be scared. But Buddy was anything but scared. He was bubbling over.

"No problem Mom; it was great. Pappy said, 'Tell your parents everything is going to be okay.'"

Pappy had died a couple of months before after a long illness that left him looking emaciated, almost unrecognizable. "How did he look Buddy?"

Buddy smiled, "Pappy looked good Mom." Buddy could hardly wait for his dad to get home that night in order to tell him the dream.

Hearing the dream, Frank had trouble controlling his tears, remembering how Pappy had taken care of him when he was Buddy's age. He and Marie both came to the same conclusion, that Pappy was now Buddy's guardian angel.

The story had all the aspects of a loved one's visit from the other side. Pappy had shown the family that he was okay. I wondered why Pappy hadn't given the message directly to his grandson. Asking Marie if her husband was a dreamer, she said that unlike Buddy, he rarely recalled dreams. Pappy had needed to speak through Buddy, whose dream channel was wide open, in order to get his message to the family. His prophetic message was cheerful, lacking any reference of what was to come.

Marie returned to checking my orthotics and gathering information for the podiatrist. Although it seemed she had finished her story, she began talking about a head injury her son had shortly after the dream. She was visibly shaken and with tears in her eyes repeated a couple of times, "I don't know why I'm telling you this." But she continued the story, saying that Buddy and his dad had been playing. Frank had been tossing Buddy up in the air, catching him and then turning him upside down allowing Buddy to slide down to their front walk where they were playing.

"Suddenly Buddy slipped—I don't know why I'm telling you this—I've got to stop—but Buddy slipped and crashed down on to the concrete walk, head first. It was horrible. We rushed him to the hospital, but the head damage was so severe they transferred him to another hospital.

"When he got there, the neurologist looked at Buddy and smiled in disbelief. 'It's like someone put his hands on Buddy's head and stopped all of the bleeding, external and internal.'

"The neurologist continued explaining that the damage to the frontal lobe could have been so severe that Buddy would have had problems with self-control, memory, and intelligence."

Marie recalled vividly how her husband almost passed out when he heard the news. She said with grave finality, "If that had happened to Buddy, I *never* would have forgiven Frank."

Marie collected herself and with a bit more composure explained that she and Frank had just watched the movie *Heaven is for Real* the day before my appointment, and that the movie had revived her feelings of the event by finally bringing to light what Pappy had been talking about when he told Buddy to tell his parents that everything was going to be okay. Pappy's prophecy had been correct. Everything was okay. Buddy healed quickly with none of the expected side-effects from a traumatic head injury.

Marie believed that somehow Pappy had been Buddy's protector. But it was only through her frantic, unrelenting need to retell the story years later that she completed her understanding of what Pappy had done. Pappy had needed to do more than protect Buddy. Pappy had needed to protect his beloved grandson and wife from emotional trauma and pain from which they never would have been able to recover. I think that Pappy is more than just Buddy's guardian angel, I think he's the family's guardian angel. I wonder what he's up to now.

EXTRASENSORY PERCEPTION

A Cop's Dreams

A COP'S DREAMS

Jill and I walked into the police station to have pictures taken for our school system's new ID cards. The powerful-looking cop taking the pictures greeted us. He wore a black net T-shirt that emphasized his muscular build and gave him the look of a young Sylvester Stallone. He got right down to business and asked for our titles that would be printed on the cards as he led us to the picture-taking area.

Jill mentioned that she was the district's behavioral consultant and asked if it made any difference that she was a part-time employee, adding as an afterthought that she had just had a baby. He didn't respond to her question, but instead responded to her comment about just having had a baby with a direct look of admiration. "Well, you'd never know it."

There was no pause between his comment and Jill's equally frank reply. "That's because I have my clothes on."

Feeling like an outsider to this unexpectedly intimate interchange, I kept quiet and waited for my turn with Anthony. No need to wait long, Jill was soon heading out the door with her new ID card.

What kind of dreams does a macho guy like Anthony have? "Anthony, I bet you get some dreams about your work."

Anthony began with an offhand description of his going through a safety training exercise designed to teach law enforcement officers how to search a building. "I knew the whole layout of the place. I saw it in a dream.

"Then there was 9/11. I was at my buddy's house in Bergen County. From his yard we just happened to be looking at the Manhattan skyline through his binoculars when the Twin Towers suddenly exploded and went down. It was horrible and reminded me of the dream I had as a kid where two tall burning buildings went down the same way. With that kind of dream, for me it's like déjà vu. They come in a deeper level of sleep and don't have anything to do with what's going through my mind or what was going on with the day. I don't bother keeping them in mind. I know I'll remember them later when I see the same thing in real life."

My ID card was ready. With appreciation for his work and impromptu sharing, I told him that I believed in angels and bet they were looking after him. Anthony's expression changed and fit his hushed tone of guarded confidentiality. It was clear that what he was going to say would be even more meaningful than his discussion of precognitive dreams.

"Strange you mention that. I went to a psychic once and she told me the year my grandmother would die and that my grandmother would send me a guardian angel. I was with my grandmother when she was on her deathbed. Just before she died she said, 'I'm going to send an angel to look after you Anthony.'" Anthony was quiet then. He had no more to say. I thanked him and headed back to school.

Once again, dream sharing had presented a far different picture of an individual than was first observed. Anthony's bravado covered a sensitivity that could leave him vulnerable. We unexpectedly met later that afternoon while he was getting a cup of coffee at the local Dunkin' Donuts. Gone was any indication of the closeness we had shared less than a couple of hours before. Anthony was a tough cop.

Like Anthony, most people are unaware of how common premonitions are. Premonitions range from the common premonition that someone is about to call us on the telephone to premonitions of disasters, sometimes personal, sometimes more general. They make themselves known in various ways including: a feeling, a knowing, a flash or mental image, and hearing words in our mind. Premonitions are considered an oddity, in part due to the fact that they aren't a routine topic of conversation. When they are discussed, it's often because of the fear of some future disaster that people with the premonitions feel powerless to prevent.

The way we respond to our premonitions is unconsciously influenced by our personality style. For this reason, premonitions that occur in dreams when our waking ego is asleep are likely to be more accurate than those experienced while awake. Like many people, Anthony gives premonitions the socially acceptable déjà vu label when they come true or become associated with a future event.

Anthony appears to be satisfied with his current ability to foresee the future in dreams. Abilities such as Anthony's, however, can be developed further. To do so, the dreamer needs to become familiar with dream patterns associated with déjà vu experiences. Identifying the dream as precognitive would allow the dreamer to be more proactive in preventing tragedies before they occur. Let's hope that if we ever find ourselves in danger, someone will show up having had a precognitive dream about the situation and be guided by an angel to keep us safe.

DO WE DREAM IN COLOR?

A junkyard is a jungle of mechanical carcasses, bicycles, appliances, and objects torn apart, some past any clues as to their original identity. The destruction results in dangerous jagged pieces of metal and combinations of scents giving the place a curious air of finality, but just the place to find an odd piece of brass to rework a home project. The Snake Hill yard was small, but what it lacked in area, it more than made up for with its high and varied piles of debris.

Next to the guard dog pen, a worker responded to my request about brass with a hand gesture, "See the boss." A narrow path led me through an outcropping of sharp metal to the shed where the boss sat at a table that seemed more like another piece of scrap metal than a work station. He silently humored me with a reply to my request with a shrug. Expecting that I would follow him he started walking to a smaller shed opposite to where I'd parked my car.

A musty barrel with odors of kitchen and bathroom devices turned out to be a gold mine for various types of brass. After getting me what I wanted, the boss started back to his desk to determine a price, again expecting me to follow. Almost past my car, he stopped and looked at the *Live by Your Dreams* business advertisement on the car's rear panel. He studied it; then studied me, and with careful deliberation pulled out a cigarette as he asked, "We dream in color?"

Pleased with the question, I began to offer an explanation, but stopped. It was as if he had said, "You think you can teach me about dreams." Still studying me and with understated assurance he said, "My dreams of the future come true in bits and pieces." After a pause of resignation he continued, "I could have avoided something." He wasn't talking to me, but was reliving an event that must have ended in destruction far worse than he was accustomed to seeing in the salvage business. A slow draw on his cigarette didn't alter the look of pain on his face. "I didn't take action." He didn't wait to hear my question about what he meant. "I don't want to think about it. People would have just thought I was crazy." He flicked his cigarette off to the side as we walked back to his worktable. He weighed the metal and charged me very little. I turned and headed back to my car.

The junk dealer had known all along that we dream in color. There must have been an unmistakably compelling color component to his dream predictions that he regretfully dismissed at the time for fear of being considered crazy. His story calls out with deadly certainty that we need to heed dream warnings regardless of what people will think.

Yes, we dream in color. Many people believe that dreaming in color is rare and are pleased to report that they do, although some people insist that they dream only in black and white. Just because we don't recall color in dreams, however, doesn't mean that we're not dreaming in color.

Dream researchers have studied a number of factors related to how we experience color including: physiological reactions to color, time spent watching black and white media, stages of dreaming, and aging. A most important factor, however, is how a person observes color in waking life. People who take notice of color in their waking lives are more likely to take notice of color in dreams. The question we need to ask ourselves is: When is it important to explore color in a dream? Like anything else, if color seems out of place, exaggerated, or simply weird, it's begging for attention. For example, if a medication is a certain color in waking life, but totally different in a dream, further consideration of the medication is warranted.

One's own associations to colors are extremely important. For example, one studying the chakras or energy centers of the body may associate the color yellow with the third chakra. The color yellow may then hold a message related to the dreamer's career or work in the world.

Black and white should also be treated as colors. If a person normally recalls dreams as being in black and white, then black and white in a dream may not be important. If the person is usually aware of color but dreams in black and white, there may be a message there about "black and white" thinking. The message could be a warning of the need to be flexible and at least see shades of grey.

THANKS FOR THINKING OF ME

Carol had been the primary administrative assistant at a school where I worked. She was always polite, efficient, obliging, and courteous. Some of her many duties included setting up appointments for staff members to evaluate children in order to determine if they needed and could profit from extra help. Over the fifteen-year period she had been with the school, she was known for her willingness to take on extra duties. One afternoon during a routine call to me, she broke down crying and said she was so overloaded with work that she didn't know what to do. It was to be over a year before I heard from her again.

Carol had resigned from her job and later obtained a similar job at another school where I worked. She gave me a call to set up an evaluation and took the opportunity to let me know what had happened. I wasn't a close friend and knowing little of her personal life, I was surprised to have a dream about her a short time later.

The dream woke me up at five in the morning and kept me awake until I had written it down.

Carol gave me a small antique music box to lubricate because it was running slowly. I lubricated it, which helped some, although it was still a bit slow. I showed it to my partner Susan and my daughter Shannon, age four. When I wasn't looking, Shannon cut letters deeply into the wooden lid making it impossible to remove them. I cried. Then I noticed that she had printed words on other things too.

Making contact with people who show up in our dreams is an important way of honoring and respecting dreams. Such contacts also provide us with opportunities to learn more about the mysterious reality of dreams. So I gave Carol a call that morning and told her that I'd been dreaming about her. I couldn't see her face, but I knew she was holding her breath and worried about what I was going to say.

Breaking the silence, I told her that in the dream she had given me a music box to repair.

I could feel relief coming through the airwaves as she replied with a noncommittal, "Oh." Feeling on safer ground, I asked if she owned any music boxes. During the brief pause that followed, I could almost see the quizzical look on her face.

"No I don't, but yesterday I was packing up some of my daughter's belongings. She's going to have a baby." Carol went on to say that she had had a good time doing a lot of reminiscing and playing with some of her daughter's childhood *musical things*. It turned out that Carol was referring to figurine music boxes, including Beauty and the Beast that played tunes from the Disney movies.

Carol was surprised and intrigued that I should have a dream that included her and what was going on in her life. In fun, she asked me to let her know if I ever get a dream with a winning lottery ticket number. Then being a bit more serious, she said that I had really made her day. "Thank you for thinking of me."

Because Carol had left her previous job on very short notice, there had been no immediate replacement for her. A number of people were angry and blamed her for the temporary chaos that took place before a new assistant was hired. It was easy to imagine that when Carol thanked me she was also thanking me for not being angry with her.

With extrasensory perception or ESP in dreams, it's tempting to examine them for additional waking life connections. Did Carol come across any childhood toys with letters scratched into them? Was her daughter going to have a baby girl?

I had recently lubricated an old music box I'd gotten for my grandchildren, but like the one in the dream, it still ran slowly. Did the music boxes Carol had played run slowly? Would they also run slowly if they were lubricated?

With detailed dreams, the dreamer needs to decide what information to investigate. Much has to do with the intention of the dreamer. Neither Carol nor I had expressed any desire to look for a deeper meaning to the dream. It would have been intrusive of me to ask any more about the personal lives of Carol and her daughter. It would have had no particular value other than to satisfy my idle curiosity.

Dreamwork, however, is self-correcting. If there had been a need for us to find a deeper meaning, either one of us might have had a subsequent dream alerting us to that need.

On the other hand, I did want to investigate the dream further with respect to my daughter. In a quick call I asked if she had ever cut letters into little boxes or had done anything like that. It was a perfect opportunity for a smile. "No Dad, I was the perfect little girl, remember?" Her delightful tongue-in-cheek response let me know that it probably wouldn't be long before she let me in on a story of her own. With that, I was content that I had honored the dream and investigated it sufficiently, allowing it to fulfill its purpose of providing a ripple effect of good will.

A THERAPIST'S PREMONITIONS

A workshop introducing therapists to the latest research and changes in mental health diagnoses drew a capacity crowd. One of the therapists—tall, broad shouldered, and muscular—was dressed in a no-nonsense brown plaid flannel shirt and jeans. His clean shaven head and deep brown eyes framed by large rimmed glasses added to an appearance that demanded my undivided attention as he approached me during the lunch break.

He had heard during our introductions that I was a dream specialist and introduced himself by saying, "Maybe you could tell me about dreams." I asked if he had any specific questions. We decided that I would begin sharing information I thought was important, with the understanding that he would stop me whenever he felt the need. As I spoke, he nodded in agreement and was soon telling me about his beliefs and dream experiences.

John worked in an inner city facility that provided counseling for juvenile offenders. The counseling was preventive in nature, an attempt to help the youths move in a direction that would lead them away from crime and subsequent incarceration. He explained how his dreams were client focused and became an alert system that would sound the alarm when the young people were in danger or were behaving in ways that would get them in trouble. As an example, John described a dream in which his clients were caught in a violent storm. Based on the dream, John spoke to the youths in an attempt to warn them that they were in danger of future arrest. The young men ignored the warning and were arrested about two weeks later.

Exasperated, John said, "I don't like to dream because all I get are warnings." Then, coming to grips with his frustration he rallied saying, "There's nothing that God doesn't tell me about in advance through dreams. It just depends on whether or not I act on what He tells me."

John began talking thoughtfully about his family members, putting pieces of information together in new ways that clarified some previously puzzling behaviors. With a smile, he recalled his mother's large collection of dream books. "She didn't talk about dreams; she would just tell me and the rest of us when we were in danger." John recognized that his own dreams were similar to his mother's and that his twenty-four-year-old son was now having similar dreams. He realized that like his mother, he hadn't spoken with his son about the use of dreams and made the decision to do so.

The conversation then came full circle back to his work with juveniles. He and I both agreed that as hard as we might try, it's difficult to get angry teenagers to listen. I suggested that in addition to warning students, he begin sharing his dreams with them, edited when necessary. Being a strong role model, the teens could be expected to follow suit and begin sharing their dreams with him. John could then form an alliance with them to figure out what their dreams meant. Before our ideas began to settle, the rapid fire, staccato voice of the workshop presenter broke through the airwaves and signaled that lunch was over.

THE BABY'S YOURS

Friday evening or not, Susan and I couldn't put off doing our laundry any longer. As we were getting out of the car in front of the Laundromat, Susan dropped a penny. A man from the next car bent down to pick it up and began talking to Susan about how pennies had changed in recent years. His comments about the reduced copper content in them caught my attention as all three of us headed in to do our laundry.

The man wasted no time introducing himself as Marco, a third-generation, Italian, blue-collar worker who was proud of his Italian heritage. He explained that people thought he was Irish because of his red hair, and that only the old Italian immigrants could recognize him as an iconic Italian. Continuing his introduction, he explained that in the past he had the dangerous but well-paying job of hanging safety cables on high girders as a part of bridge construction.

Marco was quite adept at maintaining such a rapid flow of speech without pause, even when changing topics, that there seemed no way to avoid a totally one-sided conversation without interrupting. An abrupt 180-degree change of topic can be disorienting to a person, even if he is just rambling on. Not so for this man. I intercepted him at the end of a sentence and told him I needed a dream of the future for a book of stories about dreams I was writing. I told him I wondered if he had a dream of the future he could share. My question was accepted as easily as if he hadn't been talking.

"I've always paid attention to my dreams. Ironically, I had a dream of the future that after about nineteen years just came to fruition last week. First I'll tell you the dream, then I'll tell you the story that explains it. Storytelling is a lost art you know. Television and electronic media wiped it out."

About nineteen years ago, I started having a repeating dream that I would have a daughter; I saw just what she looked like but I had a son instead.

"So, here's the story. Because I was young and didn't want to have any more children, I went to a clinic and had a vasectomy. Years later while I'm driving with my girlfriend, she tells me she's pregnant. I knew it wasn't mine. I got so mad I threw her out of the car. Just to prove it wasn't mine, I went to the doctor the next day. X-rays showed that the doctor who did the vasectomy didn't cut the tubes. They didn't tell me at the time, but because I was young, they only tied the tubes shut and somehow they got untied.

"It's now years later, my little girl has just turned seven. I was driving her and her little friends home last week. I looked in the rear view mirror and saw them sitting there—it was like looking at my dream only now it was a reality. My little girl looked the same as in the dream."

Marco went on to say, "The dream had been so moving spiritually—really high energy—that I've remembered it all these years. I stopped the car, got out my smart phone and took a video of the girls so I'd have a real picture of the dream."

Marco's laundry was finished. I had time for only a couple of questions. No, he hadn't entered into a committed partnership with his girlfriend. Although his daughter lived with her mother, Marco's ex-girlfriend, Marco had moved to less than a block away so he could develop a close relationship with his daughter. Because his former girlfriend was working, he left his job, and was living off savings and income from part-time jobs in order to be with his daughter every day when she got home from school.

I realized that I had heard a dream of the future and also an amazing story about the dream. Dreams frequently include references to the future that may be quickly forgotten. Marco's dream of the future, however, was remembered because of what he recognized in the dream as an extremely high energy. It gave the dream a spiritual significance that drove him to change his life radically. He became the committed and devoted father he might never have been without that dream.

Marco's story was captivating and provided far more information than was requested. He had not just told a dream of the future, but a story that opens the way to what every loving father dreams of, a beautiful relationship with his daughter. Marco had asked for a copy of my book when it comes out. I wonder what his daughter's reaction to the story will be? Some of her questions will be uncomfortable for him to answer. With his answers will come pain that inevitably needs to be overcome as any love deepens. But with Marco's commitment and a bit of luck, their love story may continue well into the future.

APPENDIX
Dream-Related Topics

Arthur Strock, Ph.D.

Dreaming the Future...

Sweet Dreams!

Arthur Strock, Ph.D.

ABOUT THE AUTHOR

Arthur Strock, Ph.D., is a Founding Life Member of the International Association for the Study of Dreams. He is dedicated to sharing information about the value of dreams and the practical information they provide for living our lives.

Dr. Strock holds advanced degrees in psychology and clinical social work. His professional experience includes work in hospital, corrections, school, and private practice settings. He has also taught psychology courses as an adjunct faculty member at colleges in New Jersey. His writing includes a column in the Dream Network Journal and articles online and in other publications. He currently works as a school psychologist and provides dream workshops for professionals and the general public.

Arthur resides in New Jersey with his partner, art therapist Susan Dingsor. They enjoy their rural location overlooking a natural spring-fed lake that offers relaxed kayaking during their leisure time.

DREAM WORKSHOPS

Workshops range from entertaining hour-long storytelling presentations to multi-session problem resolutions workshops. Dreamwork instruction is provided for individuals and groups in home, school, and corporate settings. For more information regarding dreams and dreaming or to contact Dr. Strock, visit his website: www.livebyyourdreams.com